Rights and Wrongs

Some Essays on Human Rights

EDITED FOR AMNESTY INTERNATIONAL
BY CHRISTOPHER R. HILL

Penguin Books

Penguin Books Ltd, Harmondsworth, Middlesex, England
Penguin Books Inc., 7110 Ambassador Road, Baltimore, Maryland 21207, U.S.A.
Penguin Books Australia Ltd, Ringwood, Victoria, Australia

—

First published 1969

—

Copyright © Amnesty International, 1969

—

Made and printed in Great Britain by
Cox & Wyman Ltd,
London, Reading and Fakenham
Set in Monotype Plantin

A PENGUIN SPECIAL

RIGHTS AND WRONGS

SOME ESSAYS ON HUMAN RIGHTS

Christopher R. Hill has been a Lecturer in
Politics at the University of York since 1966.
Born in 1935 and educated at Radley, he read
Moral Sciences at Trinity College, Cambridge,
before spending a short time in the City. He
went into the Foreign Service for three and
a half years, and in 1962 moved to the Institute
of Race Relations as Assistant Director. He
then spent 1965–6 teaching at the University
College of Rhodesia; he was imprisoned for a few
days under the Smith régime for an unknown
reason. Christopher R. Hill is the author of
Bantustans: the Fragmentation of South Africa,
published for the Institute of Race Relations in
1964.

Contents

Some Philosophical Problems about Rights

Christopher R. Hill

AMNESTY devotes itself to very specific objects – reminding the world of what most governments do to those of their citizens who step out of line on matters of conscience, finding out who are being held as prisoners of conscience, and trying to do something to improve their lot. Its task is, in other words, to tell us that there are certain rights which all human beings have, and work towards the restoration of those rights to citizens who have been deprived of them.

Four of the contributors to this volume have examined certain specific techniques of deprivation, setting out some of the ways in which people who do not conform are punished, and in the final paper Miss Cartwright outlines the progress that has been made towards international surveillance of human rights. The papers cover many parts of the world and many varieties of mistreatment; what they have in common is a belief that there are limits to the measures governments should be allowed to take in order to preserve themselves and that there are certain minimal rights of which people ought not to be deprived.

This type of belief can be – and is – held by individuals of many kinds of political and philosophical persuasion who can work happily together to further Amnesty's aims, partly because those aims are practical and partly because the organization is primarily concerned with rights about which there is little controversy. It is possible to have very decided views on, for example, the right to property, which might impede or prohibit cooperation with those who disagreed. But Amnesty's main aims are those of Articles 18 and 19[1] of the Universal Declaration of Human Rights of 1948,

1. *Article 18.* Everyone has the right to freedom of thought, conscience and religion; this right includes freedom to change his religion or belief, and freedom, either alone or in community with others and in public or private, to manifest his religion or belief in teaching, practice, worship and observance.

7

relating to freedom of thought, conscience and religion, and freedom of opinion and expression. These of course may also generate disagreement, but more, perhaps, at the level of reflection than of action. When it comes to action there is likely to be spontaneous agreement that certain situations are wrong. Thus, it is possible to hold any of a number of different views about the extremely complex questions of what exactly we mean by human rights, what those rights are, what we mean by conscience, and so on, and yet work with people who have quite different convictions. For at the practical level of working to get people out of prison it makes little difference if one man believes that the right to, let us say, freedom of speech is conferred by God, and his colleague at the next desk thinks it is a right acquired by the citizen through some form of social contract.

But though these differences of view are at one level not of vital importance, at another it is of the first importance for the individual to be clear in his own mind about what exactly he believes human rights to be. It is particularly important now, as we look back on Human Rights Year, perhaps with a dissatisfied feeling that not very much was achieved, that we should try to understand just what it is we are trying to achieve, and why.

This introductory paper, therefore, will be devoted to philosophical rather than political problems. The problems will be stated, but few conclusions suggested. I hope, though, that the paper's relevance to the far more expert essays which it introduces will be apparent.

It may at first seem pettifogging to ask 'What do I mean when I say such and such is a human right?' One, on the face of it quite reasonable, reply would be that I mean just what I say. There are certain rights which every man or woman has, just because he or she is human. To put it another way, part of what I *mean* when I say that Smith is human is that Smith has certain rights, though of course I do not have to spell all this out every time I mention Smith; nevertheless I have it at the back of my mind. If, when I

Article 19. Everyone has the right to freedom of opinion and expression; this right includes freedom to hold opinions without interference and to seek, receive and impart information and ideas through any media and regardless of frontiers.

The full Declaration is printed at the end of this volume.

mentioned Smith, I did not have this notion of rights somewhere at the back of my mind, I would not be talking about a human being, but about something else – perhaps an elephant, or a butterfly, or even a statue in the garden named 'Smith'.

This seemingly straightforward answer has some advantages. For example, it takes account of the fact that part of our complaint against governments which take extreme measures to deprive citizens of rights is that they seek to turn the victims into 'non-persons', to dehumanize them. But the answer raises serious problems. For one thing, how do I know what a person is ? Which creatures qualify, and which do not ? Presumably I do not include chimpanzees, but I do include human babies, and may include idiots. If I am a white man in Southern Africa I may exclude most Africans, on the ground that they are not fully human. There is a further problem about the dead. What do I mean when I (perfectly sensibly) say that a man has a right to a decent burial ? By the time he needs burial he will (almost certainly) be dead, and presumably no longer the possessor of rights. Perhaps the statement should be reformulated, to the effect that a man has a right *to expect* a decent burial.

What though, to return to the living, do I mean when I say babies have human rights ? There is no denying that they have some sort of rights (and that adults have corresponding duties towards them), but it seems paradoxical to assert that they have, let us say, the rights of free speech and assembly. Perhaps it would be more accurate to say that a baby will, when he reaches a certain age (but what age ?), be able, or permitted by the government, to exercise the rights he has possessed since the cradle. When I look at a baby I may think something like this (not a prediction but, as in the case of Smith, part of a definition), but when I look at a young chimpanzee my expectations will probably be rather different.

However, it may be suggested, this is arbitrary. What is it about humans that entitles them to greater rights than chimpanzees ? Let us assume for the moment that chimpanzees cannot talk: nevertheless it does not seem absurd to suggest they should be allowed the rights of free *communication* and assembly. Nor is there any obvious justification for denying them life, liberty and the pursuit of happiness – nor indeed the right to property.

Similarly, the vegetarian who reproves us for slaughtering sheep is not just saying that to kill sheep degrades men (like the argument that capital punishment should be abolished because it degrades the hangman); he is also saying that sheep have a right to life, and it is hard to detect any logical difference between this right and a man's right to life – or a mosquito's.

Our problem, then, is why we should describe certain rights as *human* rights and not the rights of all living creatures. Various answers are available. One response, it is hardly an answer, is to say: 'I'm only interested in human beings. So the question you ask may be of passionate concern to philosophers, but it concerns me not at all' – and with this there can be no argument. Another reply might be that the world and other living creatures were made for man's use, therefore man clearly has rights which other creatures do not share. This is a difficult argument to deal with, because it is very hard to see what kind of evidence would tend to prove or disprove the claim. There is also the subsidiary problem that if we say the world and other creatures 'were made' we have to postulate a maker, an hypothesis to which many advocates of human rights would not commit themselves.

The more sophisticated, and historically popular, answer would be that some rights are peculiar to man because man alone is rational. This at once raises the question of idiots. Most people would agree that they are human, but do they have human rights? An unqualified 'yes' is too simple, since often they are not capable of exercising their rights, and sometimes they have to be restrained from doing so. Perhaps therefore we should say that, just as adults have duties towards children, and perhaps animals, so the sane have duties towards idiots, and that the latters' rights are best defined in terms of those duties. This raises difficult problems about the nature of insanity, which to some extent have been tackled by psychiatrists, for example by R. D. Laing in *The Politics of Experience*, who argues that schizophrenics have not turned away from *the* real world, but simply from *our* world into another reality of their own. This is another way of expressing the thought contained in the madman's old saying: 'The world voted I was mad, and I voted the world was mad, and the world outvoted me.'

For practical purposes (and this is no answer to the philosophical problem) we must align ourselves with the majority view.

What though do we mean by rationality? It cannot just be a matter of speech, since we do not deny rationality to humans who have been dumb from birth. Nor can it be a matter of communication by other than verbal means, since it would be more or less generally accepted that animals communicate. It seems, then, that we must fall back upon some such criterion as the ability to formulate abstract concepts. The rational being is one who is able to say (to himself, if not aloud) things like 'I have a right to such and such.' We expect that the baby will eventually be able to do this, and believe the idiot would be able to if he were 'normal'. With these qualifications, we are now saying that a being has rights who is able to 'say to himself' that he has rights.

This formulation, though it sounds in some way disappointing, does seem to fit the case. It fits our intuitive notion that we are able to distinguish between those beings who are able to say this kind of thing to themselves and those who are not, whilst protecting us against the charge of anthropomorphism which may follow the assertion that animals feel pain, fear, annoyance, deprivation, in the same way as we do. If, however, it were established that chimpanzees could formulate such concepts, we might have to redraw the frontiers to allow to chimpanzees those rights hitherto reserved to ourselves.

Having made the assumption that there is a sense in which we may legitimately talk about human rights at all, we have seen that difficulties arise as soon as we try to delineate the categories of creature to whom they should be ascribed. We must now go on to ask how we may justify the assumption that human beings have rights, how we decide *what* rights they have, and what is the source of rights. We should, though, notice at this point that it barely makes sense to posit rights for man separated from society. I am not here thinking of, for example, Locke's men, who enjoy rights in the pre-societal state of affairs, but rather of the solitary who has no contact with other human beings. Robinson Crusoe, whilst he believed himself alone on his island, had no rights and no duties, except perhaps to God or himself. When he met Man Friday the first threads were spun in a whole web of rights and obligations.

Of course it can be argued that, had Crusoe remained alone, he would still have had duties to God. To the objection that if he had never been told of God's existence he could hardly have had duties to him, it may be answered that the existence of duties (and rights) does not depend upon our knowledge that they exist, or it might be answered that the knowledge of duties to God may be gained by direct revelation. The same might be said of Crusoe's duties to himself, though the notion of duties to oneself is a mysterious one, which can perhaps only be elucidated by reference to the natural law principle that it is self-contradictory not to preserve one's life. These points aside (and we shall return later to God and the natural law), we are concerned primarily with man's relations with other men, his rights against them, and duties to them.

To the first of our central questions, how we know that human beings have rights, we have already given the answer that without those rights we should not consider a creature human. This (despite the qualifications already made) is still inadequate, because we know that a great many humans are deprived of their rights and remain human. We must therefore say something to the effect that every human *ought* to be treated in such and such a way – but this does not seem to be precisely equivalent to saying everyone has such and such a right. We may therefore be obliged to say something like 'Everyone has right, because without it he would not be *fully* human, or would not be fulfilling his potential as a human being.' This is deplorably vague (though it does suggest the principle of universality) but may become more precise when we look at the possible ways in which we might discover what the 'full potential' of a human being is. With this is bound up the question of the source of rights, since of all those explanations which may be given to the first question a closely related variant may be given to the second, though the related answers need not be given to both at once.

The chief methods which have been commonly employed to discover the full potential of man are by consulting the canons of revealed religion, by studying the natural law, by discovering the will of the people, or by examining the economic system. Similarly God, the natural law, the sovereign people, or the economic system may be the source of rights. It may, however, be possible for me to answer the question 'How do I know what it is for man to achieve his full potential?' with the prescription to consult the Word of God, whilst having no other basis for my confidence that man has rights than my knowledge of the will of the people. But such a mixed position, though logically possible, is in practice difficult to sustain.

For those who adhere to a religion both questions are manageable. For the Christian the height of man's potential is illustrated in the New Testament, and from the Church he learns too that man has one overriding right, and duty, which is to act in accordance with his conscience. He is not told with any certainty what other rights he has, for different authors have given different answers, but he is at least sure of the source of this supreme right from which all others can be derived.

The natural law explanation can be adopted with or without belief in a God. In the former case natural law is held to be those aspects of the will of God which man can discover by taking thought. In the latter case man discovers principles of action by the use of reason, without reference to any higher authority. In neither case is the believer in natural law committed to the belief that all men who apply their power of rational thought to the consideration of problems will come to the same conclusions, for individual minds, like individual consciences, are unique and may reach unique conclusions. But he is committed to the central proposition that there *are* answers, discoverable by reason, if only reason is rightly applied.

To say that natural law dictates a certain belief may thus be not far removed from saying that the belief is reached by intuition, and to say this (as Benn and Peters point out in their *Social Principles and the Democratic State*) is close to saying, indeed equivalent to saying, that no further logical argument is possible. To the question 'How do you know?' intuition replies 'I just do.' More pungently, it has been said that natural law, like the harlot, is at the disposal of all men. It does at least seem clear that natural law is consistent with, and may be used as a justification for, any belief whatever. Even so, it is a type of explanation which possesses very wide appeal, for there are many who are dissatisfied with those justifications which depend upon the will of the people, or the seeming blindness of economic forces.

To discover man's full potential by discovering what the people most admire is unsatisfactory, since fashions change, and what is admired may not be what is best. But if asked how I know that X is better than Y I shall probably have either to rely upon natural law or upon some form of utilitarian ethic – that is, the belief that the goodness of an action must be measured in terms of its pleasure-giving or pain-bearing effects. But if the supporter of the will of the people is asked why he considers this a suitable criterion he too will eventually have to appeal either to natural law or to some form of utilitarianism, and even the utilitarian, if asked to justify his acceptance of pleasure and pain as the criteria of right action will, in his turn, need to rely upon natural law. Ultimately he must say 'I believe this because I believe it.'

There is an obvious sense in which the will of the people may be seen as the source of rights. That is, when the people are sovereign, and express their will in the form of laws. Clearly, the rights a man enjoys depend, in one sense, upon law or custom or both, yet the question may still be asked, why did the people choose to establish certain rights rather than others, and again a natural law reply must eventually be forthcoming. The human law, logically, is preceded by a moral judgement and to say that this judgement expresses the collective mind, or the prevailing climate of opinion, evades the question, since one must still ask how that mind, or that opinion, came to be formed.

The Marxian answer relates rights to the economic system. The central fact of society is that different economic classes exist whose interests necessarily clash. Eventually, however, there will be no classes, no conflicting interests, hence no 'rights' in anything like the sense in which we now use the word. In this final, communist, state of affairs, from which there can be no advance, man will attain his true nature. No longer forced by the exigencies of the relations of production to acquiesce in a system of rights and duties determined by those relations, he will be free to participate in a new morality which demands simply that each individual should willingly submit himself to the needs of the collectivity, playing, as in an orchestra, the part allotted to him. At this stage man will no longer be alienated from his true nature; no effort therefore will be required from him to make his act of submission; indeed, to do otherwise would be positively unnatural. Furthermore, in contributing to the collective purpose man loses nothing of his opportunity to develop his own personality and interests to the full, since in expressing his true nature he is in fact fulfilling that purpose.

In the Marxian metaphysic, then, rights in the sense in which we use the term exist only in the pre-communist stages. (They exist still in the U.S.S.R., which is a socialist, not a communist state.) For the Marxist, morality, religion, law, the state itself, are epiphenomena of the economic system, and serve the interests of the ruling class. When a rising class finds itself hampered by the entrenched beliefs of the class in power, it overthrows that class, and in so doing renders irrelevant the beliefs and institutions which went with it. It substitutes for them social arrangements suited to its own purposes, and this process of destruction and regeneration continues until the classless society is achieved. Thus the source of rights lies in the economic system, and it follows that those rights are not the expression of timeless truths concerning the nature of man, but part of the prevailing culture and liable to change as the economic power relations in society change. Rights, in this analysis, are not universal, but relative.[2]

The analysis suggests much that is illuminating. It is true, for example, that a man may often feel constrained by economic considerations not to exercise his rights. If he complains to his Member of Parliament about conditions in the factory where he works he may fear dismissal. Nor is it enough to guarantee certain basic rights, like freedom of speech, unless a measure of social and economic security is guaranteed as well. As Philip Mason has recently put it (in an article in *Race*, July 1968): 'if the lion and the lamb are equally free before the law, it will go hard with the lamb.'

2. A shining example of the relativity of some so-called fundamental rights is the disappearance of the right to own property (firmly stated in the Universal Declaration of 1948, Article 17) from the United Nations Covenants of 1966. I owe to Mr James Fawcett, Q.C., the observation that there are strong arguments against continuing to regard the Universal Declaration as the basic international instrument and for the view that it has been replaced by the Covenants, even if these do not come into force. Only five countries from the 'third world' were present to vote on the Universal Declaration, whilst 107 countries adopted the Covenants. They are therefore, Mr Fawcett argues, representative in a way the Universal Declaration never was.

Again, it is true that Declarations of Rights tend, like the Declaration of 1948, to be directed to avoiding the repetition of catastrophes which have gone before, or to exemplify the aspirations of a group which feels itself disadvantaged. It should however be noticed that just because a right is formulated by the bourgeoisie, or by the workers, and expresses their interests, this does not preclude the right in question being a human right in some much broader sense.

There is a great, and familiar, difficulty about the Marxian position. It is hard to accept that all non-economic facets of a culture are dependent upon the economic, though much easier to accept that religion, land tenure, art, marriage customs, are *related* to each other, since this does not commit one to belief in the primacy of economics. The proposition is in any case unprovable. An even more serious difficulty arises when one asks whether the proposition 'all non-economic events depend ultimately upon economic ones' is itself culturally determined. In other words, does the fact that I utter these words itself have an economic cause. If it does not, the proposition is false, since it claims universal application, and an exception has been found. If it does, it may reasonably be asked whether in some other economic state of affairs I might have uttered some quite different, and contradictory, statement. Before this question, it seems, one can only take refuge in agnosticism.

The belief that rights change and are relative to a particular society is not peculiar to Marxism. Burke, in his *Reflections on the French Revolution*, cast scorn on the whole notion of natural rights, that is, rights belonging to all men at all times as part of their nature. For him it was nonsense to talk about the rights of man; one must specify the rights of Englishmen or Frenchmen or whatever, since rights were inseparable from the society in which they had evolved, and could not be detached from that society's history and unique conditions. Burke's book was a warning to the English against the horrors of revolution, for he believed that in France the fervour of revolutionary protest had not only achieved reform (which he thought should always be gradual and undertaken with circumspection) but had spilt over into the wholesale destruction of institutions laboriously created and essential to the survival of society. Philip Mason has made a similar point (in his article already quoted). The creation of a just society, he says, carries with it great risks, for 'Every step towards reducing inequality is liable to increase resentment at what remains', and 'The very institutions that need to be done away with if society is to be just are often those which have maintained its stability.' But Mason, unlike Burke, believes the risks must be taken.

Bentham, from a point of view very different from Burke's, also attacked the idea of natural rights. He was a utilitarian who desired radical reform and believed that Declarations of Rights impeded the cause of reform, since without the force of legislation behind them they were unlikely to be effective. In a passage which is often quoted (for example by Cranston in a contribution to *Political Theory and the Rights of Man*, edited by D. D. Raphael) he said: 'Right is the child of law; from real laws come real rights, but from imaginary law, from "laws of nature" come imaginary rights. . . . Natural rights is simple nonsense, natural and imprescriptible rights rhetorical nonsense, nonsense upon stilts.'

These, then, are some versions of the view that rights are relative. If they are relative it is still logically possible that they are universal, in the sense that by extraordinary coincidence all men in all societies might possess the same rights, but it is not possible that they should be natural – part of the nature of man. In fact, of course, a moment's inspection shows that no rights are universal in the sense that they are universally enjoyed, though it may be that they ought to be universal. This, however, raises difficulties about the source of our authority for saying 'such and such ought to be the case', some of which we have touched upon in our consideration of the origin of rights. It should also be noticed that, if rights are not natural, we may, if we reproach a government for its failure to allow citizens to enjoy their just rights, be met with the riposte that the rights in question are not regarded as rights in the country whose government we reprove, and that we have no business to seek to impose our own standards upon foreigners.

The problem may be a little elucidated by consideration of the justifications societies produce for the rights their members enjoy, and the conditions under which those rights may change or be withdrawn. First, members of a society may believe that their rights and duties are adumbrated by God; in that case they will change only if such a change is believed to be in accordance with the will of God, and be withdrawn only upon terms believed to have his approval. Secondly, if rights are deducible from the natural law, they will change if sufficient members of a society have a changed perception of the natural law to produce a new consensus. In such a society the conditions under which a man's fellow citizens may deprive him of his rights will also be deducible from the natural law, and similarly susceptible to change. It may also be held that a man who fails to make right use of his reason, and so fails to perceive the natural law, has only himself to blame. Thus for Locke slavery is a 'moral fault', since it is perverse not to follow the rule of natural law that a man does not voluntarily surrender his liberty.

Thirdly, one may adopt some variety of contract theory. According to this, states owe their origin to a social contract, the parties to which agree to entrust to a government some of the rights and duties which they would otherwise have had to exercise for themselves. Here, rights change if the contract is dissolved and a new one entered into, or if a clause is added to the existing contract. Rights will be withdrawn from anyone who is judged not to have kept the bargain he entered into.

These views may be illustrated with reference to any crime – let us take murder. The deist or the natural law theorist will know, either from the word of God or introspective assessment of the natural law, that the penalty is death. But in new conditions fresh inspection of God's word or a new assessment of the natural law may suggest that the punishment should be reduced to, let us say, life imprisonment. The contract theorist, on the other hand, will argue that the penalty may only change if the contract is altered; such an alteration will require a decision by the citizens and the passing of a law, and their decision will presumably be based either on utilitarian arguments or upon intuition.

This discussion points to the questions of the relation of rights to government and to law. The individualist idea was that government was good if it was cheap, provided security and justice, and otherwise left the citizen alone. This idea is by no means out of date: it informs our attachment to what may be called the 'traditional' rights of freedom of speech, religion and so on which are based upon the feeling that the individual should be left alone, provided only that he does not infringe his neighbour's right. Part of the duty of government is to see that the individual, whilst remaining free, does not make it impossible for the next man to exercise his own freedom.

However, as Fawcett has aptly said (in his contribution to *Political Theory and the Rights of Man*, edited by D. D. Raphael): 'But this classical framework of civil and political rights, while it provides society with some essential securities, can leave it morally immobile. The man who stole bread was sure of a fair trial and was free to speak out in public against the law that condemned him, but he was still hanged.' Not only do moral perceptions change; cultural conditions change too. In a society where no one could read or write it would be nonsense to claim the right to a free press, but as resources increase, so do our expectations. Nowadays, therefore, in addition to the traditional rights, we tend also to expect a further set of economic and social rights, different in kind from the traditional ones. These include the rights to education, work, medical care, leisure, perhaps even holidays with pay. But, whereas it is relatively easy to form the opinion (leaving aside the question of the logical basis of the opinion) that the traditional rights ought to be universally acknowledged, it is far less easy to hold so firmly to the view that the 'modern rights' have similar claims to universality. Even the traditional rights would probably not be demanded in all circumstances: the utilitarian may have to admit that sometimes a degree of repression is not only necessary, but even desirable, and the believer in natural rights may reluctantly admit, in circumstances of exceptional emergency, that rights must be sacrificed. When it comes to the modern rights, which demand not just forbearance on the part of governments but also action to achieve certain ends, it is hard to avoid the conclusion that rather different considerations must apply. We may of course *assert*, for example, the right to education, but we can hardly expect a government to give effect to that right unless the country possesses sufficient resources, and we are prepared to tolerate a degree of governmental control of those resources, sufficient to enable it to provide the service claimed.

It seems, then, that in some cases we ask governments to acknowledge the obligations they already have, and in others to undertake new ones. Mrs May, for example, argues that the right to freedom of conscience should be *recognized*. In her view the right can be logically deduced from the right to freedom of thought, conscience and religion contained in Article 18 of the Universal Declaration of 1948. I am myself not entirely convinced about this. Clearly, if there is a right to freedom of conscience it must allow one to propagate opposition to a law, otherwise the notion would be empty. But freedom to disobey the law is another matter, and to determine the conditions under which disobedience is permissible is the classic dilemma of those who have tried persuasion and failed. Explicit discussion of this dilemma lies outside the scope of this paper, but some of its possible resolutions are implicit in the earlier discussion of the origin of rights and the basis of our views about the nature of man.

There are a number of other verbs, apart from 'recognize', that we may attach to rights. We may agree upon them, as was done by those who framed the Universal Declaration. We may discover them by reflection. We may demand or assert them. We may set up machinery (as Miss Cartwright shows) to protect them, or we may respect them without the sanction of machinery. All these formulations (and one could think of many more) carry different overtones, ranging from those implying the belief that rights are inherent in the nature of man to those consistent with the view that they are relative to a particular society. Our choice of word therefore is not unimportant, since it may reveal our underlying beliefs about the nature of rights.

We have assumed throughout this paper that rights imply duties; one cannot exist without the other. We have still to ask, for any given right, who exactly has the corresponding duty. If a baby has rights, of whom may he claim them? Here it seems that his primary claim is against his parents, then against his other relations. He has a claim of a different kind, and of far less intensity, against any adult, and in rich states where orphanages can be afforded he has, if all else fails, a claim against the state. This illustrates the way in which, as states become richer and more developed and governments take wider powers, acts which were formerly perceived as charitable are now seen as acts of simple justice.

An orphan in the old days (in England) was cared for by a charitable institution. He was lucky, and he was constantly reminded of it. The poor man, if he fell ill, was, if he was lucky, taken port wine jelly by Lady Bountiful. The bright boy, if he was very lucky, gained a university scholarship. Now the baby, the poor man and the student all receive care paid for by their fellow citizens and administered by the state, and all perceive what they are given as a right, not a charity.

Thus governments have acquired the duty to do what they can for their citizens, but they do not have a similar duty to the citizens of other countries, with the exception that, it is often argued, former colonial powers have a duty to their former colonies. If, however, the British Government sends a donation towards the relief of flood victims in Turkey it is not thereby acknowledging a day-to-day duty, but making a charitable gesture which it is under no obligation to repeat.

So it appears that citizens have certain kinds of claim which they direct primarily at their own governments, and if government is unable to help them, at their fellow-citizens. If neither source can provide adequate assistance, they may direct appeals to foreign governments and foreign individuals, accepting, though, that foreign governments have no binding duty to respond and that foreign individuals will probably wish to think first of their own compatriots. Even if a right may be claimed *for* all men, it may not be claimed *of* all men.

Clearly these dividing lines are not sharp. Sometimes a government may properly be said to have a duty (quite apart from such obligations as those imposed by treaties) to assist another, and very often the citizen of a prosperous country may feel bound to aid the starving abroad. But he will feel it less incumbent upon him to educate them, and much less to attempt to provide holidays with pay, unless he is committed to a programme of international revolutionary action which he believes will produce such desiderata as by-products.

As well as not feeling a strong call of duty to assist in bringing about certain states of affairs, I may think that the effort is unlikely to be successful. There is little chance of bringing about a return to liberal democracy in Albania or taking industries to the bushmen of the Kalahari. Nevertheless, even if the achievement of such conditions is not practicable, because the governments concerned are unwilling or unable to bring them about, I may think that the conditions ought to be enjoyed by all men. In that case I may think that the advantages of industrial society are a human right which should be worked towards everywhere, even if in any places there is not much likelihood of their being achieved.

We may perhaps usefully employ the French distinction between the rights of man and the rights of the citizen. There may be some rights which I think should be acknowledged as belonging to all men because they are men, and which I believe should be respected by all men and all governments. There may be others which I think can be ascribed only to the citizens of certain countries, and not to the citizens of others. These will be rights in some countries, where social conditions are appropriate, but not in others. The test will not be whether a creature is human, but whether he possesses citizenship of a particular country.

Some rights are guaranteed by law, and the citizen whose right is infringed has his remedy in the courts. But it must not be forgotten that, even in a country where courts are uncorrupt and judges impartial, the law itself may impose barbarous penalties which the judges are not at liberty to set aside. Nor does equality before the law imply that all must be treated in exactly the same way. Apprentices and master craftsmen have different rights, which the law will uphold, but both have a right to equal consideration by those who administer the law.

Many rights and obligations rest not upon law but upon custom, and as customs change (perhaps gradually, perhaps abruptly in response, for example, to the shock of colonial contact) so will the rights and obligations be modified. There are cases too, particularly where the traditional rights are concerned, where a right exists just because there is no law. As Hobbes said, where the law is silent, the citizen is free – though this is not as reassuring as it at first sounds, since for Hobbes law was equivalent to the expressed will of the Sovereign, and there was no *earthly* constraint upon his expressing it whenever he wished, and upon any subject.

On the whole the area where the law is silent covers the more traditional rights like life, liberty, free speech and freedom of worship, which do not need positive promotion by governments, though they need safeguarding with penalties for those who infringe them. The newer rights, as we have seen, demand positive action by governments, and many of them require considerable governmental control of resources.

The traditional political and civil rights do not imply that all men are politically equal, with an equal right to participate in the political process. It is perfectly possible to uphold all the first twenty articles of the Universal Declaration (perhaps with the exception of the first, which asserts that all men 'are born free and equal in dignity and rights') and yet retain a society in which very few citizens have the right to vote, and where very great social and economic differences exist. The newer rights, on the other hand (Articles 21 to 28), do specifically include the provision (Article 21) that 'everyone has the right to take part in the government of his country, directly or through freely chosen representatives', and go on to a series of social and economic prescriptions, which though not specifying equality, would, if achieved, tend to produce a society in which social and economic differences were greatly reduced.

In very many societies, indeed in all, it seems reasonable to hope that the traditional rights may ultimately be achieved. They enshrine what are often called 'Western values', an arrogant description if the West thereby sets them over against the values of the socialist East (for what was Marx if not Western ?), and the wish that they may spread may be seen by some as disreputable cultural imperialism. Their great advantage is that they are cheap – they require a sufficiency of policemen and judges and the will to respect them, but not much else. Bearing in mind all the philosophical difficulties underlying the whole terminology of rights, it is possible to say that these traditional ones are in some sense 'universal'.

It does violence, however, to common sense to use 'universal' in the same sense when we talk about the modern social and economic rights. There is at least one obvious sense, as Cranston (*Political Theory and the Rights of Man*, edited by D. D. Raphael) has pointed out, in which they *cannot* be universal. Let us take his example, the right to periodic holidays with pay (Article 24). Clearly, this can only apply to people who work, and though everyone has the right to work, not everyone is compelled to. (Indeed, if a small child exercises his right to work, the humanitarian may protest). Since there are in fact a great many people who, by reason of age, ill-health, or simply disinclination, do not work, it seems perverse to assert that they have a right to holidays with pay. If this is so, the right cannot possibly be universal. Furthermore, many of those who do work are unable to take any holidays at all – there may be no one else to milk the cow. All this suggests that Article 24 ought to be rephrased to the effect that people who are in regular paid employment ought to be able to take periodic holidays with pay, and with such a formulation few would quarrel. A similar argument can be applied to the right to form and join trade unions (Article 23).

But if rights of this kind are not universal or natural, what are they? It may perhaps be said that they are *aspirations* and for this view there is some support in the opening words of the preamble to the Universal Declaration: 'The General Assembly proclaims this Universal Declaration of Human Rights as a *standard of achievement* [my italics] for all peoples and all nations. . . .' This, though, seems to be negated by the beginning of Article 2: 'Everyone is entitled to all the rights and freedoms set forth in this Declaration, without distinction of any kind. . . .' As Cranston says, 'a right is not the same as an ideal; the words have different meanings.' Nor is it the same as a purpose or an aspiration. Nevertheless, it does look as if the modern rights are nearer to ideals, purposes or aspirations than to rights of a traditional kind and may, by their impracticability, tend to bring the whole notion of rights into disrepute.

A way out may be simply to admit that the same word is used in everyday language in at least two quite different senses. But although the senses are quite different at the extremes, they do shade into each other. There are some rights about which we are not quite sure whether they are natural, or goals. Education may be one of these: 500 years ago few would have said there was a natural right to schooling; now the matter is at least open to question. There is, then, an area of uncertainty, and rights have developed through time. At one time our 'traditional' rights were themselves new; now much of Thomas Paine's defence of human rights seems self-evident, though to some of his contemporaries it was revolutionary, and to Newman too dangerous for undergraduates. Thus it looks as if we may be forced back upon the view that something is a right when it is seen as such by enough people (but how many?). This is unsatisfactory, because it means finally abandoning the principle of universality, but it may be the best we can do.

What is clear is that for many workers in the cause of human rights the old civil and political rights are a sham without the social and economic ones. This view is capable of wide variation; some would say simply that it is not much good giving a man freedom of speech if he has not enough to eat. Others would say that the social and economic rights are of such importance that if the reconstruction of society, and with it the loss of the older rights, is necessary to their achievement, that it is not too high a price to pay. Others of course have the new society as their chief aim, and are not primarily interested in rights.

It is, too, often said that the traditional rights are only allowed so long as their exercise does not threaten the state very seriously. In time of war something like Britain's Regulation 18B may be necessary, and from this it is sometimes concluded, with dubious logic, that the rights are a sham even in time of peace.

The conflict between the notions of rights as natural, and as standards to be achieved, is only too apparent in much writing on the subject. The Universal Declaration itself is so framed that part of it seems readily consistent with the first interpretation, and part with the second. The division is so obvious as to suggest that a more satisfactory, and more honest, solution might have been to produce two separate Declarations. The General Assembly did indeed decide in 1951, when discussing a Covenant which it was hoped would eventually be accepted as binding by member states, that it would instead bend its efforts to the formulation of two Covenants. The secretary-general (quoted by Fawcett, *Political*

Theory and the Rights of Man, edited by D. D. Raphael) summed up:

that civil and political rights were enforceable, or justifiable or of an 'absolute' character, while economic, social and cultural rights were not or might not be; that the former were immediately applicable, while the latter were to be progressively implemented and that, generally speaking, the former were rights of the individual 'against' the state, while the latter were rights which the state would have to take positive action to promote.

In 1947 Unesco carried out an inquiry into the theoretical problems raised by the Universal Declaration (on which work was then in progress), and some of the papers were published in 1949 under the title *Human Rights.* Many of the contributors emphasized that human rights could only be stated in relative terms, others were exercised by what they saw as a need to synthesize the traditional 'Western' approach with the newer preoccupations of the socialist bloc; nearly all saw that these two approaches were dissimilar, though the solutions offered differed greatly.

One way of dealing with the problem was to employ phraseology capable of many different interpretations. For example, Arnold J. Lien, an American political scientist, wrote of human rights:

In their quintessence they consist basically of the one all-inclusive right or enabling quality of complete freedom to develop to their fullest possible extent every potential capacity and talent of the individual for his most effective self-management, security and satisfaction. In this one transcendant human right, all others are implied, or, of it, all others are phases, each receiving a position of prominence or an emphasis dependent upon the particular temper or trend of the times.

This formulation at least has the advantage of all-inclusiveness; it seems to be consistent with almost any solution, including Lien's own view that human rights are universal 'attaching to the human being wherever he appears, without regard to time, place, colour, sex, parentage or environment'.

Others went bald-headed for the socialist solution. For example, Luc Somerhausen, Director of the Secretariat of the Brussels Senate, believed that rights could not be fully enjoyed in a society based on the profit motive, and therefore on exploitation. Traditional bills of rights had in his view been concerned with 'man the egoist'.

When the Unesco committee of experts came to draft their conclusions they did not avoid the ambiguity which some contributors, indeed, had seen as a necessary, or even desirable feature of any document which hoped to command wide support. Their working definition of a right was 'a condition of living, without which, in any given historical stage of a society, men cannot give the best of themselves as active members of the community because they are deprived of the means to fulfil themselves as human beings'. This, again, is consistent with almost any philosophical view, but the committee's justification was that it was more concerned to obtain agreement on what rights exist, and on action, than to reach a doctrinal consensus.

Some of the rights the committee defined show its members' difficulties only too clearly. For example, the right to live is described as the foundation of all others, but the committee went on to say: 'All rights derive, on the one hand, from the nature of man as such and, on the other, since man depends on man, from the stage of development achieved by the social and political groups in which he participates.' Here an appearance of precision is obtained by amalgamating the 'natural' and the 'relativist' views in one sentence.

Of the right to work the committee said: 'The right to work implies the right of the workers to participate in the collective determination of the conditions of the work, as well as the right of the workers to understand the general significance of the work done.' The assertion of such a plainly false implication nicely illustrates the difficulties facing a committee composed of members from widely differing ideological backgrounds.

Finally, the committee held that 'the right to live finds its most complete manifestation in the life of thought and in the various modes of artistic and scientific expression'. This, if meaningful, seems a prime example of academicians' arrogance.

We have already glanced at the difficulties of interpreting the social and economic rights contained in Articles 22 to 28 of the Universal Declaration. There is one additional curiosity which should be noticed, and that is the right to education (Article 26).

Not only is there a right to education, but 'elementary education shall be compulsory'. To make the exercise of a right compulsory is unusual (though not unique: for instance, the exercise of the right to vote is compulsory in Australia) and raises problems. For example, if a grown man who has never received any education is sent to school against his will he may protest that he has a right *not* to be educated. We may answer that, if he does not go to school he will not reach his full potential as a human being, but what if he disagrees, or simply does not want to reach his full potential?

The way in which the traditional rights may be incorporated in a socialist constitution and altered over time may be illustrated by reference to the 1950 and 1968 Constitutions of the German Democratic Republic (a fuller account of which is contained in the *Amnesty International Review*, August 1968). The traditional right to emigrate was present in 1950, but in 1968 had been replaced with: 'Every citizen of the G.D.R. has the right to move freely within the state territory of the G.D.R. within the framework of the laws.' Most of the familiar rights, to freedom of conscience, religion, personal liberty and so on, and of the newer ones, are still present, but they have to be read alongside the provision that 'the most important driving force of socialist society is the identity between social requirements and the political, material and cultural interest of the working people and their collective groups'.

The new preamble, too, is very different. In 1950 it read: 'The German People, imbued with the desire to safeguard human liberty and rights, to reshape collective and economic life in accordance with the principles of social justice, to serve social progress, and to promote a secure peace and amity with all peoples, have adopted this Constitution.' The 1968 preamble refers rather extravagantly to the G.D.R.'s responsibility 'of showing the whole German nation the road to a future of peace and socialism', attacks American-led forces of imperialism, which, in concert with West German monopoly capitalism, have split Germany and concludes: 'imbued by the will to continue unswervingly and in free decision on the road of peace, social justice, democracy, socialism and international friendship, [the people of the G.D.R.] have given themselves this Socialist Constitution.' Thus, though the Universal Declaration may be a useful guide to legislators and makers of constitutions, it may give inspiration in a variety of directions.

In conclusion, it must be admitted that, though those imbued with 'Western' values may see socialist interpretations as perversions, there is some truth in the socialist point that liberal democratic Bills of Rights only allow the exercise of freedoms so long as they do not endanger the basis of the state. Miss Cartwright quotes the European Convention, which provides that freedom of opinion and expression 'may be subject to such formalities, conditions, restrictions or penalties as are prescribed by law and are necessary in a democratic society' and the purposes for which restrictions may be imposed are so wide that they would probably be acceptable to, let us say, the South Africa Government. However, as Miss Cartwright says, the dangers of abuse will be much reduced if an independent judicial body decides when legislation is repugnant.

I have attempted in this paper to touch upon some of the problems of political philosophy which bear upon the question of human rights, and so upon the work of Amnesty. To raise questions is not the same activity as to answer them and I have attempted to do no more than point towards some possible answers. But even if, at the level of reflection, one remains in doubt, agnosticism is no excuse for inaction. We do not, whenever we hear of a case of injustice, mistreatment or governmental excess, sit down and work out why it should evoke some reaction from us. We just react. Pity, fear, human sympathy, the feeling 'there but for the Grace of God go I', all sorts of reasons, lead us to send off a parcel of blankets to a prisoner, give a donation to a relief fund, write a letter to *The Times*, or whatever the appropriate action may be. The point, at this level, is that something is done.

Thus it is not *necessary* to consider philosophical problems before taking up the cudgels on behalf of those who are deprived of their rights, any more than it is necessary for the lover of the countryside to ask himself whether it was made by God. But though action may be immediate, thought has its place in the life of any rational being. By contemplation action may be stultified – or it may be greatly enriched.

Deportation in South East Asia

Malcolm Caldwell

There are many techniques for dealing with awkward citizens. The quickest, and in some ways the most effective, is simply to kill them. A somewhat less drastic method is to remove them by deportation, and it is because this method is so obviously shocking that we have placed Dr Caldwell's paper first in the group of those dealing with specific techniques of repression.

We are more shocked, though perhaps we ought not to be, by the murder of thousands than by that of a lone individual. Similarly, we are more shocked by mass deportations than by isolated cases. Dr Caldwell discusses large-scale deportations in South East Asia, where the victims are regarded, generally on racial grounds, as posing otherwise insuperable political and social problems. He goes on to consider the deportation of individuals whom governments label as agitators or politically undesirable, and in so doing shows that the removal of an individual solves a quite different question, and has a different sociological explanation, from the problem which is solved by a mass deportation. But he also shows that the method is equally effective, and unjust, whether applied to the individual or the mass. – C.R.H.

DEPORTATION is a terrible punishment. Forcibly uprooted from a familiar environment and expelled to an alien one, the victim of deportation faces the prospect of never seeing the country of his birth or choice again. Frequently the tragedy is heightened by separation of the deportee from his wife and family. Clearly deportation is one of the harshest sanctions available to any government for application against those subject to its jurisdiction. Historically, it has been the fate of many distinguished people and countless anonymous ones. In the modern world it is still, unfortunately, all too prevalent. In this essay, the subject of deportation is not dealt with in a comprehensive or systematic way.

What I have done is to illustrate the subject by reference to a number of specific instances of deportations drawn from a restricted period – the recent past – and area – chiefly South East Asia.[1]

It happens that deportations, some on an unusual scale, have been a recurrent feature of the post-war South East Asian scene. For this there are good historical reasons, rooted in the colonial past. Since the earliest times of which we have any kind of record, Chinese and Indians have been visiting, and occasionally settling in, the region. But it was during the period of European dominance that their influx became marked and their presence more definitely permanent. By 1956 ethnic Chinese constituted 5·6% of the population of South East Asia and ethnic Indians 0·9% – in numbers 10·3 million and 1·7 million respectively. Distribution of these immigrant communities was very uneven. For example, in the Federation of Malaya in 1956 38% of the population was Chinese (2·3 million), while half of all the Indians in the region were concentrated in Burma. Both Chinese and Indians also tended to congregate in the towns and cities. Four-fifths of the population of Singapore was Chinese in 1956, and half the population of Bangkok. No important change in these generalities is required to bring them up to date, except in so far as absolute numbers are concerned (the population of the region, alien[2] and indigenous alike, has been growing since 1956 at a rate of 2·5% per annum).

Local resentment against the immigrant minorities has two sources. Racialism is one – reaction to the out-group with its different ways and values. The other is economic. Under colonial

1. South East Asia consists of: Burma, Thailand, Laos, Cambodia, North Vietnam, South Vietnam, Malaysia, Singapore, Indonesia, Portuguese Timor and the Philippines.

2. A note on usage: throughout this essay I have used 'alien' as an adjective in a wider sense than 'alien' as a noun. Whereas in the former case I have used the word in the sense of 'foreign *in origin*' as well as 'belonging to another country', in the latter I have restricted the usage to 'a non-naturalized foreigner'. Thus 'alien communities in Indonesia' would embrace all those ethnically and culturally Chinese, Indian, Arabic, etc., while 'Indonesian aliens' or 'aliens in Indonesia' would simply refer to those of the above communities who had not become naturalized Indonesian citizens. In other words, I have used 'alien' adjectivally as virtually interchangeable with 'immigrant' ('coming into a country from abroad to settle there permanently'), while I have used the noun 'alien' in its narrower technical sense.

rule the indigenous social systems of South East Asia underwent great stress, and many cherished features of pre-colonial life shrivelled or disappeared. A few local people were able to capitalize upon the new opportunities afforded by the Western presence. For the majority, living standards fell during the period of most intensive colonial exploitation, from the 1870s to the 1930s.

In this disruptive and exploitative process the alien minorities played a significant part. They were attracted or deliberately imported by the colonialists to fulfil certain essential functions – such as providing a pool of cheap labour for Western enterprises, undertaking lower-grade clerical and supervisory jobs, and acting as economic go-betweens. In the latter capacity the Chinese and Indians were especially liable to arouse animosity, for it was they who brought the money economy, with all it entailed, down to the village and face-to-face level: buying 'native' produce to start it on its way, via the local ports, to the industrialized countries; selling the imported manufactured goods of the industrialized countries; lending cash to 'money-hungry' peasants who now needed it to pay colonial taxes and to buy the products of Western capitalism.

Profits accruing to immigrant traders and money-lenders as a result of transactions with the local peoples were inevitably seen by the latter as a measure of their own exploitation. Moreover, all the accumulated hatred of colonialism tended to be vented also on its alien Asian 'agents', whom ex-President Sukarno of Indonesia described as a 'second layer of colonialism'. Since they were also more accessible, familiar and vulnerable than the actual representatives of the colonial power, the Chinese and Indians from time to time during the colonial period bore the brunt of local discontent and wrath (for example in the anti-Indian riots which wracked Burma in the nineteen-thirties). The control of the local economies acquired by the Chinese and Indians under colonialism persisted into the post-independence period after the Second World War. All the frustrations that accompanied the gradual revelation that political independence by itself would not bring general economic prosperity found a ready focus in this continuing 'second layer of colonialism'. Throughout South East Asia it was tempting, politically, for the new leaders consciously to incite xenophobia, in order to divert popular attention from their own failings as administrators and planners. It was also economically tempting to fleece the minority groups, by special taxes or outright expropriation. Unfortunately, such tactics had a good deal of popular support. People everywhere show an inclination to respond more readily to crude appeals to their prejudices and apparent self-interest than to reasoned statements of the real causes of their troubles.

With this much as background, we may now turn to a consideration of some cases. Since Indonesia is far and away the largest country in South East Asia – accounting for roughly half the population and area – and since the problem with which we are concerned has assumed perhaps its most serious proportions there, it will be convenient to start with it.

The Chinese had been visiting Indonesia for many centuries before the advent of Dutch power. But it was only with the rapid increase in economic opportunities under the Dutch, and in particular in the nineteenth and early twentieth centuries, that the influx became considerable. Today, ethnic Chinese in the country probably number some two and a half to three million (the statistics are imperfect and there are problems of definition) – roughly one in forty of the population. Having established a position of ascendancy in many sectors of the economy during the colonial period, the Chinese were well placed to take whatever economic advantage might accrue from the departure of the Dutch. Indonesian nationalists had different ideas, of course. When it was found by experience that the Chinese were too well entrenched to be budged by straightforward economic competition, recourse was had to other measures, such as banning certain lucrative lines of business to them. In a series of enactments and regulations, culminating in those of November 1959, the Indonesian Government subjected the Chinese to continual harassment, with the support and blessing of many Indonesians – especially devout Muslims who found certain features of Chinese life and values objectionable to their religion.

Under the 1959 regulations, an effort was made to prohibit aliens from engaging in retail trade in the rural areas, a sector of the economy in which the Chinese had a near monopoly. In some parts of Indonesia the Chinese were physically evicted and evacuated to urban areas with great harshness on the part of the authorities. Many were repatriated to China – 96,000 it is estimated between December 1959 and December 1960.

Despite all the attempts that were made to exclude them from profitable economic activities, the Chinese continued to show great ingenuity in circumventing regulations and in building up profitable businesses. It ought to be made clear that although it was the overt wealth of the Chinese that engendered local hostility, the majority of Indonesia's Chinese inhabitants were in fact poor labourers and petty traders (a parallel situation would be that in Europe vis-à-vis the Jews and popular attitudes towards them). The riches of the big Chinese tycoons were all the more conspicuous and blatant in the context of the floundering Indonesian economy, which deteriorated more or less steadily through the late fifties and early sixties, inflation and shortages inflicting great hardship on the people.

The laws governing Indonesian nationality are complex. In 1960 China and Indonesia ratified a Dual Nationality Treaty. Before that year some local Chinese had become Indonesian citizens under prevailing arrangements, but the vast majority had not. Now those of the latter group who wished to acquire Indonesian citizenship had to take certain positive steps to do so, or automatically lose their dual status and Indonesian nationality with it. The Chinese community was already clearly split into two communities: those born in Indonesia, often from families that had been in the archipelago for generations (known as Peranakan); and those more recent, China-born, immigrants and their families (Totok). It is therefore impossible to state simply what the present legal position of 'the Chinese' in Indonesia is, for there are many gradations. There are those who are fully assimilated, with Indonesian names, Indonesian relatives and Indonesian citizenship. But at the other end of the scale there are those who are citizens of the People's Republic of China and proud of it. According to the Indonesian authorities there were over 1·1 million citizens of mainland China in Indonesia at the end of 1965, though only about a quarter of them possessed Chinese passports or equivalent documents. Just under a million Chinese were believed to have attained Indonesian citizenship by that time. This would leave over half a million Chinese in an ambiguous position – some stateless, some with sympathies for and/or connexions with Formosa, some simply untouched by bureaucracy.

All this is to some extent of little account, since by an all too familiar mechanism the Chinese tend to be popularly regarded as one community, equally subject to resentment whether they try to keep themselves apart or whether they try to assimilate. A complicating factor is the existence of a communist régime in China, for the Communist Party of Indonesia (P.K.I.), although it had massive and overwhelmingly non-Chinese support, also provoked violent antagonism – particularly from the strong Muslim organizations. The hostility generated in the first place by the 'alien' ideas of the pro-Peking P.K.I. took in as its target the Indonesian Chinese as well, because of the common link with China.

Anti-Chinese disturbances erupted sporadically before 1965, but it was after the coup of that year that the situation began seriously to deteriorate. President Sukarno had long sought to avoid a showdown between Indonesia's communists and the predominantly right-wing army, correctly surmising that it would be a bloody affair. When the army in fact seized power in October 1965, its leaders seized the pretext of an attempted pre-emptive coup by left-wing junior officers to institute a massive slaughter of communists and sympathizers. The Chinese were inevitably caught up in this catastrophe. Some were P.K.I. members, but the great majority were not. Some Indonesians obviously took the chance presented by this legitimized blood-letting to settle personal scores with Chinese into whose debt they had fallen. All this could be accomplished under the blanket allegation 'once a Chinese, always a Chinese', with its sinister implication of links or sympathies with the People's Republic.

Deportation readily occurred to the new right-wing leadership as a possible solution to the minority problem. Already rich Chinese were streaming out of the country. For the poorer there was no such option. From many parts of Indonesia they had simply been expelled, their shops looted and houses burned down behind them. The already crowded Chinese quarters of bigger towns and cities – such as Glodok in Djakarta, the capital – had perforce to absorb the further flood of rural refugees.

All Chinese were forcibly evicted from Atjeh in Sumatra, a stronghold of devout Islam. These refugees were herded into improvised camps – tobacco sheds, dilapidated mosques and temples, local Chinese schools – in and around the port of Medan. Conditions were, by all accounts, deplorable. An article in the *New York Times* magazine (23 October 1966) described 500 Chinese 'surrounded by boxes, bedding and anything else they could hurriedly bring with them' quartered in 'a vast but flimsy tobacco shed' near Medan: 'The air in the tobacco shed was hot and heavy, the cross poles for drying tobacco creaked and strained under the unaccustomed weight of cooking utensils and laundry.' A Chinese 'sat cross-legged on a stool in a 6-by-10-foot area allotted him, his wife and five of their eight children'. The eldest daughter lay on a couple of crates, shaking with fever. Detainees awaiting deportation were subjected to harassment and provocation by Indonesian youth groups, especially students of the right-wing action group K.A.M.I./K.A.P.P.I. Philip Koch of the Australian Broadcasting Commission reported on 19 November 1966 that K.A.M.I./K.A.P.P.I. students had broken into the camps to beat up Chinese refugees, and that local (Medan) Chinese were frightened to go out into the streets. The authorities appear, however, to have tried to restrain these anti-Chinese actions (although it was the military themselves who forcibly entered the Chinese consulate in Medan on 18 January 1967 to lower the Chinese flag). As a result of incidents a number of Chinese were arrested, including forty-one young people who were jailed for six weeks, during which time they claim to have been beaten and tortured. When the forty-one eventually reached China they were acclaimed as heroes. Officially, they – like their fellow detainees – were 'repatriated'. Most of them had been born in Indonesia, however, and therefore could not technically be *repatriated* to China. The same consideration applies to a large, but indeterminable, number of the others 'repatriated' from Indonesia to China.

The numbers involved in and around Medan are conjectural. About 8,000 Chinese were expelled from Atjeh. The process of shipping them out to China has been a slow one. Only one ship appears to have been involved – the Chinese S.S. *Kuang Hua*. The statistics of embarkations known to me are:

3.9.66	1,005	Chinese
20.11.66	1,076	,,
29.1.67	1,070	,,
6.5.67	1,099	,,
Total	4,250	,,

According to those arriving in China, 'thousands' still awaited repatriation at that time, midway through 1967. The *Observer* reported (18 February 1968) that 3,000 were still waiting in the Medan camps then, eight or nine months later. But other estimates put the number very much higher – one source claiming that 26,000 Chinese are detained in the Medan area. Some recent reports suggest, however, that conditions in the camps may have improved somewhat, with the inmates permitted to grow food for themselves on patches of waste land.

What was the fate of the deported Indonesian Chinese on arrival in China? According to Hsinhua, the Chinese news agency, the first shipload were settled in Kwantung province, on the Yangchun overseas Chinese forestry farm. The second group went to the Chuan Shang state farm in Ninghua county of Fukien province, and the third to the Tunghutang overseas Chinese farm in Ningteh county of Fukien province. It will be noted that the refugees from Indonesia have been resettled in suitable areas. Chinese immigrants to Indonesia came almost entirely from Kwantung and Fukien provinces. As far as Sumatra is concerned, the principle Chinese groups represented are the Hokkiens and Teochius, from southern Fukien and north-eastern Kwantung respectively. For those born in Indonesia, climate must also be an important factor in adaptation to the new environment in China. Sumatra straddles the Equator. The Tropic of Cancer crosses Kwantung, while Fukien is just to the north. There are, of course, parts of northern China which would be very foreign to Chinese born and brought up in Indonesia.

The Atjeh expulsions have perhaps attracted most attention in the West, partly because of the violent incidents which they sparked off, and partly because of the acrimonious exchanges which developed out of them between the governments of China and Indonesia. But for the Indonesian Chinese the situation has also been serious elsewhere in the archipelago. Kalimantan – Indonesian Borneo – has, for example, been the scene of mass expulsions. West Borneo has the highest percentage of Chinese inhabitants of all the provinces of Indonesia. It is there that the main troubles in Borneo have arisen.

Estimates of the number of Chinese in Kalimantan vary. An official estimate of 1956 gave 271,000 for West Borneo. At prevailing rates of population growth this could well have risen to nearly 400,000 in the interim. An Indonesian army spokesman recently put the number even higher – at half a million, of whom, he thought, only 100,000 had become Indonesian nationals. Many Chinese in Borneo are engaged in peasant agriculture, and many more in rural trade. Reports in 1966 and 1967 indicated that it was official policy to move the Chinese from the rural areas into or near to the major towns. The reasons behind this were twofold: first, to enforce the 1959 regulations prohibiting aliens from engaging in retail trade; and second, to facilitate security operations against armed communist guerrillas. The latter aspect of the matter was – and is – of interest to authorities on both sides of the border, since armed bands also operate in Sarawak in Malaysian Borneo. In both cases support and supplies for the guerrillas are alleged to come from the local Chinese.

Early reports indicated that large numbers of Chinese were being moved from the border area, and that Chinese families from other rural areas were being re-grouped in and near the principal towns, either doubling-up in existing Chinese-owned property in these towns or being put in emergency refugee camps. Some Indonesian spokesmen talked of 'repatriating' all the non-Indonesian nationals among the Chinese, but others said the numbers involved were small, and that these wanted to go 'home' to China. Whatever their real intentions, the Indonesian authorities evidently did not envisage providing the shipping to carry these people 'home' to China.

Reports from West Borneo in 1967 presented a confused picture. A number – the figure 600 was quoted – of Chinese were said to have been jailed for pro-communist activities. Thousands more had certainly been moved to the towns, and especially the ports, with the major concentrations in and around Pontianak. Then, in November 1967, the process was suddenly accelerated by a bloody pogrom of Chinese at the hands of local Dyaks. In this slaughter more than 100 Chinese were reported to have been killed and a further 40,000 driven from their homes (*Observer* 18 February 1968). After the massacres, all those Chinese who had not already fled the interior were reported to have been expelled. This must have involved the movement of huge numbers of people, and certainly strained the resources of the regroupment areas. About 450 Chinese were reported to have died in over-crowded emergency camps in the coastal towns of Pontianak and Singkawang in February. Meanwhile, the expulsion of Chinese from the interior had produced a critical economic situation. Without Chinese traders, none of the forest produce, including rubber, could be moved, and without Chinese peasant farmers rice production fell sharply, giving rise to fears of widespread hunger, if not worse.

It is clearly impossible for the Indonesian authorities to 're-patriate' or deport the hundreds of thousands of Chinese inhabitants of Kalimantan, far less the three million of Indonesia as a whole. Deportation, as we shall see, *can* be effective in the case of an individual, or at most a small group of people, but is an inappropriate way of tackling problems of the magnitude of that posed by the Indonesian Chinese. The Soviet deportations of small minority national groups – the Crimean Tatars, the Volga Germans, the Kalmyks, the Karachai-Balkars and the Chechen-Ingushs – during the war affords no parallel or model, since movement here was inside one country. One of the problems faced by Indonesia and some of her neighbours today in dealing with the indigestible portion of the alien minorities is precisely where to deport them to.

Although China, as we have seen, has admitted some thousands of deported Indonesian Chinese, there is no evidence that she is prepared to open her doors indefinitely, quite apart from the intractable logistical problem of moving hundreds of thousands by sea. On the other hand, hundreds of thousands of the Chinese in Indonesia are anti-communist and inclined to support the Taiwan régime, and would certainly most strenuously resist 'repatriation' to mainland China. Nor can one imagine China making them welcome. What, then, of Taiwan ?

The Taiwan régime has opened contacts with Indonesia's new rulers which would have been impossible in the Sukarno era, when – especially latterly – close diplomatic relations were established with Peking. It is said that the Taiwan authorities have offered to help the Indonesian government to weed out communist agents among the Indonesian Chinese. But there has been no indication that they are prepared to accept significant numbers of Indonesian Chinese into Formosa itself.

Apparently plausible alternatives that have been mentioned in the context of the plight of the Indonesian Chinese are Hong Kong and Singapore. But a moment's consideration should dispel the illusion that comfort is to be had from these quarters. Both places, admittedly, are virtually Chinese city states. But both already suffer from overcrowding, from steep rates of population growth, from unemployment, and from consequent underground communist activities. The security forces in both would certainly refuse to admit any Indonesian Chinese suspected of communist sympathies. Already it has been reported (Melbourne *Herald*, 16 March 1967) that the Singapore government had refused entry to a number of Chinese refugees 'from a neighbouring island' – probably Sumatra. Lee Kuan Yew, the Prime Minister, has made sympathetic noises, but he is not seriously in a position to open Singapore to unlimited Chinese immigration from Indonesia. Nor are the authorities in Hong Kong.

Elsewhere, a number of Chinese from Indonesia can certainly be absorbed, but once again in insignificant numbers compared with the magnitude of the problem. Among those voluntarily leaving Indonesia since the position deteriorated, countries of destination have varied widely – from the neighbouring Philippines to West Germany, where 40,000 are estimated to have settled.

As far as Indonesia and her neighbours in South East Asia are concerned, this problem of alien minorities – a complex hangover from colonialism – is made doubly difficult by the special role important sections of the minority groups play in the economic life of the countries concerned. They certainly cannot be replaced in the short run. This is so self-evident that caution and discretion have been forced upon the Indonesian authorities. Furthermore, there are signs that those powers – chiefly the Western capitalist countries and Japan – who now, since the 1965 right-wing coup, wish to aid the country economically in order to create a good climate for private foreign investment, are urging restraint upon the Indonesian leaders in their tackling of the problem of the economic power of the local Chinese.

Minority problems arise from the diffusion of mankind throughout the planet, a process which began with human history itself. But with the world's recent rapid population growth mass movements of peoples, whether voluntary (migrations) or involuntary (deportations), have ceased to be feasible. The numbers now involved defy transportation, while at the same time there are no more remaining lands that are both hospitable to human life and comparatively devoid of it. This is a truth which has to be faced not only by the Indonesians, but also by the peoples of all other countries finding difficulty in assimilating alien groups and immigrant minorities.

It is time now to turn to another aspect of the uses of deportation. Capitalism and colonialism disturbed earlier population patterns in a vigorous, indeed violent, way, both in instigating the acceleration of overall population growth rates, and in encouraging massive redistributions of population over the surface of the globe. But capitalism and colonialism also provoked a profound reaction of rejection of their excesses, not least in the colonized countries. What appeared as patriotism or radicalism on the part of those opposed to colonialism appeared of course as subversion or plain criminality in the eyes of the authorities. The 'agitator' or 'hired agent of international communism' of the Special Branch men might well be someone sufficiently inspired by idealism and altruism in pursuit of the goal of freedom to have given up normal family life and all chances of materialistic self-advance. Whatever the truth of the matter, a favoured way of dealing with such 'trouble-makers' was deportation. Malaya, now Malaysia, and Singapore provide cases in point.

The inter-war depression hit Malaya very badly. Colonialism had produced a totally distorted economy in which the efficient supply of a handful of primary commodities required by Western industry dominated everything else. When the prices of these commodities suddenly collapsed, as a result of the seizing-up of the economies of the West, the Malayan economy collapsed as well. Rubber tappers and tin miners were thrown out of work. No provision was made for their relief or re-employment. They wandered the country providing for themselves as they might, or huddled in the cities. The trade union and wider labour movements were in their infancy.

Not surprisingly, the distressed thirties saw changes, including a sudden upsurge in radical and labour activity. One of the prominent agents in this stirring was the Malayan Communist Party (M.C.P., founded in 1930), though it ought to be made clear that Party intervention followed rather than preceded labour discontent as revealed by strikes and other forms of protest. A local reporter was told by angry strikers on a rubber plantation in 1937 that the communists were not responsible for work stoppages, and that they resented being accused of being communists simply because they banded together to obtain improved conditions (*Straits Times*, Singapore, 29 March 1937). Nevertheless the general labour unrest provided an environment and context in which social radical movements such as the M.C.P. could sink roots and build, proving the worth of the party by its practical usefulness in disputes and in such matters as organization and education.

The major part of the wage-earning labour force in Malaya was immigrant – Chinese and Indian principally. Not surprisingly, therefore, social radical impulses spread most rapidly through these communities, whose circumstances of life were more directly affected in an adverse way by the depression than were those of the prevalently Malay subsistence farmers and feudal-bureaucratic employees. This concentration of radicalism in the alien communities of course afforded the British colonial administration an important security weapon – deportation.

Few Chinese or Indians were citizens during the colonial

period. Citizenship was open only to those who could claim that both parents had been born in Malaya, and naturalization was restricted to those who had lived in the country for fifteen years. The British authorities made it standard practice to pick up suspected 'agitators' and labour organizers and to deport them. As far as the Chinese were concerned, this amounted – in practice – virtually to a death sentence, since communism was at the time outlawed in China, and on arrival there the deportees from British Malaya and Singapore were shot out of hand (see, for example, the *Straits Times* of 28 October 1929). The British official resort to deportation marched parallel with the growth and effectiveness of the M.C.P. The party was under continual pressure from the security forces. It was not registered, and was therefore an illegal organization, the members of which were liable to arbitrary arrest and imprisonment, or to deportation under the Banishment Ordnance. In 1937, for example, twenty of the party's top leaders were picked up and deported.

In a different category from political deportations was the voluntary repatriation of unemployed immigrant workers, though this too had political aspects. It was one way, for instance, of exporting unemployment and therefore of shirking the challenge of providing alternative employment or welfare support from public funds. It was opposed by some employers who regarded a pool of unemployed labourers as vital to the economy, in that it enabled wages to be depressed to bare subsistence levels, but on balance employers agreed with the administration that vast numbers of workers without jobs or money would constitute a serious risk to Malaya's stability and an all too fertile seedbed for 'agitation' and 'subversion'. When the depression overtook the Malayan economy, therefore, assisted passages were offered to out-of-work Indians, and, on a minor and more restricted scale, to some out-of-work Chinese. In the three years 1930, 1931 and 1932 nearly 200,000 Indians and over 75,000 Chinese were thereby helped to return to India and China.

The war and Japanese occupation produced a temporary lull in the British struggle against 'subversion', though in aiding the predominantly Chinese communist anti-Japanese guerrillas inside Malaya the British exercised due circumspection lest they compromise their post-war options. After the war, the reappearance of labour unrest led predictably to suppression, culminating in the 'Emergency', which lasted from 1948 to 1960.[3] Once again, deportation became a tool of official policy. In the early stages of the 'Emergency', whole Chinese villages were swooped on by the security forces, including units of the British regular army, and their inhabitants interned prior to 'repatriation'. From January to October 1949 over 6,000 Chinese were thus interned, of whom 700 had been shipped to China by April 1950. Chinese communist sources claim that, in all, 35,000 Chinese were deported from Malaya by the British authorities from the beginning of the 'Emergency' in June 1948 to the end of 1950. However, there were estimated to be nearly half a million Chinese squatters in the rural areas (where the guerrillas – mostly Chinese – operated). It was obviously not going to be possible to deal with the problem of their active or passive support for the guerrillas by deporting them all. China had accepted the hundreds whom the British had deported (the communists controlled the ports of southern China by the end of 1949) by going along with the fiction that they had themselves sought voluntary repatriation. But half a million was a different matter – once again leaving aside the logistical obstacles. British policy underwent a change on perceiving these truths. Instead of deporting the rural Chinese squatters, 423,000 of them were rounded up into 'New Villages', which were fenced in with barbed wire and guarded, until, at a later stage, with the defeat of the guerrillas, they could be transformed into peaceful settlements.

However, deportation did remain a selective sanction in Malaya and Singapore, both under the British and latterly after the granting of independence. The successor independent régimes retained – and retain – attitudes towards communism and 'agitators' inherited virtually unchanged from the colonial authorities. It might seem *a priori*, that the granting of political independence was bound to have radically altered the situation and thus have deprived the anti-imperialist left of any possible grounds for

---

3. See my 'Subversion or Social Revolution in South East Asia' in M. A. Jaspan and Michael Leifer (eds.): *Nationalism, Revolution and Evolution in South East Asia*. Hull Monographs on South East Asia, forthcoming.

reasonable dissent. Why this is not the case requires a word or two of explanation.

By withholding the vote from most of the Chinese, by over-representing the backward and conservative rural areas, and by effectively preventing the left from participating in the elections, Britain was able to transfer political sovereignty to local leaders representative of the most conservative social forces, and amenable to perpetuation of significant – indeed vital – economic privileges for the ostensibly retiring colonial power. Britain – aside from the important political influence she retained through 'expatriates' in key positions in the administration – kept a secure grip on the local economy, owning and controlling, with but slight concessions to other overseas interests, all the tin-dredges, three-quarters of the large rubber estates, almost all the oil palm estates, some two-thirds of Malayan foreign trade, and many of the newer industries. Moreover, Britain retained the right to station troops, harbour warships, and house military aircraft in the 'independent' country.

So there were immediate grievances for the radical nationalist to voice. Moreover, the structure of the economy led inevitably to extremely uneven development, with a mainly urban minority benefiting from the private foreign investments, while in the Malayan rural areas rapidly expanding population in a context of antiquated socio-economic institutions and relationships spelt depressed living standards. But even the superficial prosperity of the big towns and cities was deceptive, for the capital-intensive foreign enterprises could absorb no more than a fraction of the numbers coming year by year on to the labour market, and the result was serious and growing unemployment. The conservative Alliance government in Malaya and the rightist social democrat P.A.P. administration in Singapore were both committed to development by private, mainly foreign, investment. But this entailed the remittance abroad as profits, dividends, salaries of 'expatriate' managers, etc., of a major part of the locally generated capital, thus depleting the capital available for domestic economic development. In these circumstances, radical nationalist criticism of the *status quo* was inevitable.

Where and when encountered, it was – and is – met with a ruthless efficiency inherited from, and indeed still to some extent directly influenced by, the British. The Special Branches of Malaysia and Singapore are rightly regarded as models of their kind. One of the advantages they enjoy is that the local citizenship laws are of such complexity as to allow of their abuse in cases where the authorities wish to be rid of a political opponent considered a 'trouble-maker'. For example, residence qualifications can be so stringently and formalistically interpreted, when the need arises, that temporary periods outside the home state – to attend university in a neighbouring state for example – will be deemed to violate the requirements, however frequent visits home have been in the interim. Deportation is frequently resorted to as a follow-up to alleged or technical breaches in the case of political 'undesirables'.

A recent case involving deportation illustrates the hardships involved for the victims. Low Tai Thong was arrested in 1956 as a political suspect in Singapore. Although a review board recommended his release in 1962, this recommendation was never in fact carried out, and he remained in prison. Early in 1967 Low was served with an expulsion order, but this was not executed at that time. However, in May 1967 he was actually deported to China, after eleven years in jail. It is not clear under what legal power this deportation was carried out. On arrival at a Chinese port, he was refused entry – at his own request. Returned to Singapore, he was detained and served with a Banishment Order, since it was argued that he was a non-citizen trying to enter the country without permission (Low was born in Sabah, north-west Borneo).

Banishment Orders are normally confined to those convicted of criminal implication in secret society activities – to gangsters in fact. Low Tai Thong, therefore, is now, at the moment of writing (May 1968), being kept under criminal prisoner conditions. He has been offered his liberty if he will renounce his political beliefs. His family and friends have explored every avenue in an attempt to secure his release, but to no avail. Amnesty International has also taken up the cudgels on his behalf.[1] An Amnesty group has

1. Low Tai Thong was released on Sunday 16 March 1969 after the British Foreign Office had intervened on his behalf. On release he came to Britain.

offered to bear all expenses if he is released and allowed abroad to study. So far the Singapore and Malaysian government have remained impervious to criticism and appeals.

It is not always easy to determine the facts of cases involving detention and possibly deportation in this region. For instance, in answer to a question about deportations on political grounds asked in the Malaysian Dewan Ra'ayat (House of Representatives) on 11 June 1968 the Minister of Home Affairs claimed that the figures for persons deported between 1948 and 1959 were 'not readily available'. He added that from 1960 to 1965 inclusive there were no such deportations, but that in 1966, 484 Indonesians were repatriated to Indonesia, and in 1967 a further 137. But the whole question is, what is meant by 'deportations on political grounds', for deportations or banishments with an underlying political motive may be concealed by dealing with the offenders as criminals and deporting them as such under the sweeping powers of the Internal Security Act. It is to be feared that Malaysian and Singaporean Chinese and Indians, in particular, will continue to run the risk of deportation or banishment on covert political grounds.

Singapore is a predominantly Chinese city in which a large but naturally declining proportion of the population was born abroad (in 1957 it was estimated that half the adult Chinese population resident in Singapore had been born in China). The Chinese constitute roughly one-third of the population of Malaysia. Indonesia houses three million Chinese. In the neighbouring Philippines the problem is on a minor scale, but still thorny, and has once again involved deportations.

In 1955, 133,000 Chinese were registered with the Philippine Bureau of Immigration as aliens. But the community whose members would regard themselves as Chinese is certainly much bigger than that – it has even been put as high as half a million (the total population of the Philippines is about thirty million). Despite continuous official discouragement and hostile regulations, Chinese have been settling in the archipelago for many centuries. Economically, they have come to exercise an influence out of all proportion to their numbers. Just before the Second World War, Filipino Chinese controlled over 70% of retail trade, owned 75% of the rice mills, and had a virtual monopoly of rural trade and commerce.

But this very success has made of the Chinese community in the Philippines one of the foci of Filipino nationalism and – as in Indonesia – a mass of legislation has been introduced in an attempt to wrest economic power from their hands. In 1954 a law was passed aimed at the exclusion of aliens from retail trade. Further measures have narrowed other economic opportunities open to the Chinese.

Simultaneously, strenuous efforts have been made to choke off further Chinese immigration. The annual immigration quota is now fifty, and illegal Chinese immigrants from Taiwan are, if caught, unceremoniously bundled out of the country. For those Chinese already resident in the Philippines, regulations governing naturalization and acquisition of citizenship are tough, and rigidly enforced. For example, a Chinese applicant must show that all his children are enrolled in state schools where Philippine history, government and civics are taught. In one case where naturalization was rejected, of the Chinese applicant's nine children, eight were properly enrolled in state schools in the Philippines, but one was being educated in China (at an English school). Historically, the children born in the Philippines of Chinese fathers and Filipino mothers were regarded as Filipinos. This position was changed in 1947, when it was ruled that such children did not acquire Philippine citizenship.

The relevance of all this to deportations is direct. Aliens may be deported for a variety of political and economic offences. The economic offences include such vague offences as 'profiteering' and 'hoarding'. Evasion of import controls – smuggling is common in the Philippines – carries with it, for the alien caught in the act, the automatic penalty of immediate deportation 'without the necessity of further proceedings on the part of the Deportation Board' (Section 20 of the Import Control Law of 1949). It is perhaps fortunate for some that corruption is as prevalent as smuggling in the Philippines. Nevertheless, the regulations providing deportation for economic offences by aliens have been enforced on many occasions. For example, President Quirino rejected an appeal against a deportation order on thirty-three

Chinese convicted of 'profiteering in prime commodities' in 1951 and the sentence stood.

Deportation has also been employed in the case of political offenders. A well-known case here involved brutal separation of man and wife. William Pomeroy, an American who had been stationed in the Philippines during the war, returned there after the war and married Celia Mariano, a Filipino. Both were involved in the post-war left-wing Huk rising, and in 1952 were captured and sentenced to life imprisonment. In 1962 the sentence was commuted, but the authorities deported Mr Pomeroy while simultaneously refusing his wife permission to leave the country. After a prolonged fight, Mrs Pomeroy was eventually allowed to leave the country and rejoin her husband. The human tragedy in cases such as this requires no stressing here.

Burma's minority problems were partly solved by the Second World War, for at that time thousands of Indians flocked out of the country ahead of the invading Japanese. Most did not return after the war. However, the resident Indian minority continued to attract hostility in independent Burma. Like the Chinese elsewhere in the region, the Indians of Burma had come to dominate certain sectors of the economy. As money-lenders before the war, they had taken over a third of all cultivated land as a consequence of mortgage foreclosures. Since they were prepared to accept lower wages than the Burmese, Indian coolie labourers monopolized most urban wage-earning jobs. Indians owned nearly 30% of the rice mills. The inter-war depression greatly exacerbated economic tensions between the communities, and racial riots were of frequent occurrence.

In the period of anarchy at the outbreak of the Pacific war, thousands of Indians fled the country by a number of difficult and dangerous routes through Tamu, the Naga Hills, the Hukong Valley, and Maungdaw and Buthidaung in Arakan. Thousands perished in swamps, quicksands, jungles and inhospitable mountains. British sources estimated that half a million Indians left at this time, about half of the known Indian population of Burma in 1940.

After the war, independence came quickly to Burma, and in the first year of sovereignty, in 1948, a Land Nationalization measure was enacted. Further measures sought to switch ownership and control of economic assets and profitable commercial opportunities from Indian to Burmese hands. It was made difficult for Indians to become citizens, and even the successful in this respect found that full rights were still denied them. From March 1962, with the advent of the army Revolutionary Council, a series of nationalization measures was inaugurated which brought almost all economic activity in the country under state control, and therefore deprived many Indians of their former livelihood. Starting with major categories such as oil, mining, rice and timber, the Burmese government went on to nationalize insurance, export and import trade, internal distribution of key consumer goods, and some categories of shops. The nationalization of shops, in March and April 1964, particularly hit local Indians. Their position was rendered even more precarious by the refusal of the Burmese government to renew various kinds of licences for Indians, or to renew their Foreigners' Registration Certificates. Many Indians had already left the country when, in the middle of 1964, repatriation began in earnest. So far about 160,000 Indians, including persons of Indian origin born in Burma, have been repatriated to India. The circumstances surrounding the mass exodus make it clear that most of those involved are more accurately to be regarded as deportees, and as in deportations elsewhere in South East Asia provide many cases of great hardship. In addition, much of the wealth of the Indians, fixed and liquid, was appropriated by the Burmese authorities, and the question of assets left behind in Burma by repatriated Indians is still under discussion by the governments of India and Burma.

With these observations, I conclude this survey of the uses of deportation, with particular reference to South East Asia. With the passage of time, as the new nations settle – one way or another – the most pressing of their minority problems, deportation is less likely to figure so prominently on the local political scene. However, in the immediate future there seems every likelihood that deportation will continue to add its quota of personal and familial tragedies from year to year.

Banning in South Africa
A Technique of Repression

G. Naudé

Banning in South Africa, unlike deportation, is a technique of some subtlety. It is directed not to the physical removal of the person banned, though this is sometimes a by-product if the victim finds life unbearable and decides to leave South Africa on a one-way ticket, but to the silencing of his voice.

The South African Government says, in effect, that certain of its opponents are no longer fit to remain of the community, though they are permitted physically to remain in it. In this respect banning is more like excommunication than ostracism. Heresy is not stamped out, but its propagation is effectively controlled.

As this paper shows, banning is far from humane. It leads to all kinds of human misery, spreading far beyond the actual individuals who are banned. But, it may be argued, it is less inhumane than execution or deportation, and it is less efficient, because banned people do still retain some minimal contact with other human beings. Why then does the South African Government put up with this, admittedly small, degree of inefficiency?

Part of the answer must be that there is a propaganda value in being able to point out that in South Africa 'subversives' are not killed, nor even necessarily imprisoned. This is useful propaganda not only outside the country, but for satisfying the consciences of white South Africans at home. Of course, most people are effectively prevented by fear from associating with the banned, but there are still some South Africans who, although foreigners to Europe, retain some European notions about human rights, and may be offended if too many fellow-whites are too violently mistreated. Banning can be presented, and is eagerly accepted, as a necessary and relatively mild way of dealing with dangerous infections.

Banning silences discordant voices, and in so doing it turns persons into non-persons. This in turn reinforces the community of fear which is white South Africa. For what more effective warning, what more powerful incentive to keep out of trouble could there be than the presence in the same town, perhaps the same suburb, or even the house next door, of a shadow who was once a person?

This is emotional language, but it is the kind of language which people who have been banned have to use to express their feelings, as those who have read some of the books listed in the bibliography at the end of this article will know. – C.R.H.

SINCE 1948, when the Nationalist Party in South Africa came to power, until the end of 1967, 807 South Africans of all races have been 'banned'.[1] Nine have died, a few have had the banning orders withdrawn, some have left the country. But for the majority, banning has meant their being completely cut off from the social and political life of the community. They are not seen at any social function or at a meeting of any kind; those under 'house arrest', the severest form of restriction, cannot go beyond their garden gates without first obtaining the written permission of their district magistrate. They have been utterly silenced. No statement they have ever made, no statement they might make during the period of their banning order may be published. The banned include the most prominent and the most militant leaders of organizations that oppose the government's apartheid policies.

Being deprived by a banning order of his liberty has a catastrophic effect on the individual; the effect of the removal of 800 individuals from public life has had far-reaching effects on hundreds of others. Banned persons who were members of non-political societies, such as the National Council of Women, of purely charitable organizations, even of sporting bodies, cannot attend their meetings or take part in their affairs. Patients cannot be attended by the doctor of their choice if, being banned, he is restricted to an area other than the one in which the patient lives; those awaiting trial cannot be defended by the lawyer in whom they have confidence if, being banned, he is not allowed to appear in court. Students and pupils have suffered when their teachers, being banned, can no longer carry on with their profession. But

1. S.A. Institute of Race Relations, Survey, 1967, p. 39.

the most serious effect of the banning of so many government opponents has been to hamper the struggle for a free, democratic, liberal South Africa. This, of course, is what banning is intended to do.

How has the government been able to neutralize its opponents so effectively? Who are the banned – these people who live 'half-lives', who have been rendered 'unpersons'? What has been their reaction to their restrictions? What has been the reaction of the society as a whole?

To supply the answers to these questions we must return to the election of 1948. The National Party won, but it did not have the country behind it. Together with the Afrikaner Party, it won 79 seats to the 71 of all opposition parties. But the Nationalists and the Afrikaner Party together polled only 443,719 votes to 623,530 of the opposition. This has been explained as being largely due to 'the general though not entirely consistent tendency to weight a rural vote considerably more than an urban one'.[2] At that time, Afrikaans-speaking, National Party supporters predominated in the country districts, English-speaking, United Party supporters were concentrated in urban centres. The majority of the electorate did not vote Nationalist. The electorate consisted of Whites, males and females, and Coloured males. African men, in the Cape Province only, were voters, but in 1937 had been placed on a separate roll. They were entitled to vote for four White members to represent them in the House of Assembly, and their election took place at a different time from the general election of May 1948. They returned Mr Sam Kahn, a leading member of the Communist Party, in November, and in doing so they could hardly have shown their opposition to the Nationalists in a more effective manner. The majority of the inhabitants of South Africa were voteless – that is, African men in the Transvaal, Orange Free State and Natal Provinces, all African and Coloured women, and all Asians. They did not support Nationalist policies.

The most militant opposition was, of necessity, extra-parliamentary. It came from the Communist Party, the African National Congress, the South African Indian Congress, the

2. Carter, 1958, p. 152, citing a memorandum by Advocate Suzman to the tenth Delimitation Commission, in 1952.

Liberals, the Non-European Unity Movement, the Springbok Legion (an ex-servicemen's organization), trade unions with mixed memberships, students, outspoken clergymen.

To force its apartheid policies on the country, the National Party had to forestall the possible future formation of a united front against it of all these groups. It had to destroy these organizations. It did not have the power or sufficient support to outlaw them all at once, it had to proceed slowly. It decided, together with other methods, to make extensive use of the technique of 'banning'. It took powers to ban individuals, to ban meetings, to ban the press, and finally to ban the organizations.

The Minister of Justice was given powers to ban individuals by administrative action. In this way, he could lop off the leaders of any organization, one by one, render the organization ineffective in its protests, and do all this in a perfectly legal manner. These powers were linked with an anti-communist drive. It was easy to sell anti-communism to the White electorate. Under cover of the Suppression of Communism Act, 1950 (Act No. 44 of 1950), which outlawed the Communist Party – the only party at that time which stood for universal franchise and equal rights for all, irrespective of race or colour – the Minister was given power to curtail the liberty of an individual, to prohibit him from belonging to organizations or attending meetings. He could do this if he, the Minister, 'deemed' that such a person was furthering the aims of communism. No proof was required. No charge, trial or conviction was necessary. And the definition of communism was made very wide.

The definition was so wide that the Johannesburg Bar Council commented: 'The objects of Communism as defined in the Act are very wide indeed. They include many liberal and humanitarian objects which are advocated and cherished by persons who are very far from being Communists.'[3] The special correspondent of the *Cape Argus* predicted that if the provisions of the Act were strictly applied, 'many thousands of citizens will, to their infinite surprise, find that they are Communists'. (23 February 1951)

Banning has, indeed, covered a wider and wider range of people.

3. Cited by Bunting, 1964, p. 167.

Initially it was used against members of the Communist Party and prominent trade unionists. When the Bill was being discussed in Parliament, the Communist Party warned that its powers would not be limited and that in the end anyone at all might be banned. It called for united opposition to the Bill. But each section of the community feels safe until one of its own members is affected. Today, bans are issued against ministers of religion, city councillors, parliamentary candidates, society women, members of the legal profession, eminent professors, scientists, writers, and so on. And bans are being issued by the score against Africans endorsed out to remote, isolated rural areas, merely for the purpose of intimidation.

Here is the long, involved and novel definition of communism as defined in the Act:

'communism' means the doctrine of Marxian socialism as expounded by Lenin or Trotsky, the Third Communist International (the Comintern) or the Communist Information Bureau (the Cominform) or any related form of that doctrine expounded or advocated in the Union for the promotion of the fundamental principles of that doctrine and includes, in particular, any doctrine or scheme –

(a) which aims at the establishment of a despotic system of government based on the dictatorship of the proletariat under which one political organization only is recognized and all other political organizations are suppressed or eliminated; or

(b) which aims at bringing about any political, industrial, social or economic change within the Union by the promotion of disturbance or disorder, by unlawful acts or omissions or by the threat of such acts or omissions or by means which include the promotion of disturbance or disorder, or such acts or omissions or threat; or

(c) which aims at bringing about any political, industrial, social or economic change within the Union in accordance with the directions or under the guidance of or in cooperation with any foreign government or any foreign or international institution whose purpose or one of whose purposes (professed or otherwise) is to promote the establishment within the Union of any political, industrial, social or economic system identical with or similar to any system in operation in any country which has adopted a system of government such as is described in paragraph (a); or

(d) which aims at the encouragement of feelings of hostility between the European and non-European races of the Union the consequences

of which are calculated to further the achievement of any object referred to in paragraph (*a*) or (*b*);
'communist' means a person who professes to be a communist or who, after having been given a reasonable opportunity of making such representations as he may consider necessary, is deemed by the Governor-General or, in the case of an inhabitant of the territory of South West Africa, by the Administrator of the said Territory, to be a communist on the ground that he is advocating, advising, defending or encouraging or has at any time after the date of commencement of this Act, advocated, advised, defended or encouraged the achievement of any of the objects of communism or any act or omission which is calculated to further the achievement of any such object.

The definition of 'communist' was extended in 1951 (Suppression of Communism Amendment Act, No. 50 of 1951) to include anyone who had, *before* the introduction of the Act, advocated, advised . . . communism, and anyone who had belonged to, or actively supported any organization, outside the Union, that had as its object, or one of its objects, the achievement of communism, etc.

The generally accepted definitions of communism and communist as given by the Oxford English Dictionary (1961) are:

Communism is a theory which advocates a state of society in which there should be no private ownership, all property being vested in the community, and labour organized for the common benefit of all members; the professed principle being that each should work according to his capacity, and receive according to his wants. A communist is an adherent of the theory of Communism.

In terms of section *two* of the Act, the Communist Party was declared to be an unlawful organization. A liquidator was appointed to take possession of and dispose of its assets, etc. Section *four* provided for the drawing up of a list of former officers, office-bearers, members and active supporters of the Communist Party by the liquidator. Mere attendance at a meeting convened by the Communist Party before it was outlawed could be construed as active support. For the rest of his life in South Africa the victim of this interpretation is subjected to special persecution as a 'listed' person. For example, he must notify the police of any change of address or change of employment or he commits an offence. Listed persons have lost their employment for no reason other than that the Special Branch police have warned their employers of the inadvisability of employing them.

The Minister's powers to ban are contained in sections *five*, *nine* and *ten*.

Under section *five* he could order a person whose name appeared on the liquidator's list to resign from membership, and not to take part in the affairs of any organization specified in the banning order, nor to become a member of Parliament, or the Provincial Council or any other public body specified. A proviso restrained the Minister from ordering sitting members of Parliament to resign unless a Select Committee, appointed for the purpose, found, after investigation, that they were communists in terms of the Act. In 1954 this section was amended to give the Minister power to prohibit a listed person from attending any gathering in any place during a period specified in the order. 'Gathering' was defined to mean any gathering of any number of persons having a common purpose. In 1962 this section was further amended to extend the meaning of 'gathering' to include any particular gathering or any gathering of a particular nature, class or kind. (Act No. 76 of 1962.)

Section *nine* empowered the Minister to prohibit any person (not necessarily a 'listed' person) from attending any particular gathering, or prohibit the gathering itself from being held if, in his opinion, the objects of communism would be furthered either by the attendance of such person or by the holding of such meeting.

Section *ten* enabled the Minister to prohibit a person from being within any area specified in the notice served on him if he, the Minister, considered that such person was advocating the achievement of any of the objects of communism by being in such area. In 1962, this section was amended by giving the Minister power to impose a prohibition on a person's absenting himself from any specified area, from communicating with any person or receiving any visitor, and by instructing such person to report to the police at specified times. (General Law Amendment Act, No. 76 of 1962.)

The above amendment, in simple language, gave the Minister

power to impose 'house arrest'. The area from which a person was prohibited from absenting himself could be his home, as in the case of Mrs Helen Joseph, or a flat, or a kraal in an African Reserve, as in the case of the African whose banning order we reproduce below. The area, or place, was defined to include any premises, building, dwelling, flat, room, office, shop, structure, vessel, aircraft, vehicle, or any part of such place or area.

The penalty for breaking any of the orders served under sections *five*, *nine* or *ten* was up to a maximum of three years in jail, without the option of a fine. The penalty for advocating communism was a prison sentence of up to a maximum of ten years without the option of a fine.

The Communist Party dissolved itself just after the third reading of the Bill. But Mr Sam Kahn, a very sharp thorn in the flesh of Nationalist Members of Parliament, was still in the House. A Select Committee was duly appointed, and duly found that he was a statutory communist in terms of the Act. He was expelled on 26 May 1952. Undeterred, the African voters of the Cape elected Mr Brian Bunting, also a former member of the Communist Party, to take his place as their representative in Parliament. The same procedure was followed in order to expel him, and the African voters then elected Miss Ray Alexander, a former member of the Communist Party and an outstanding trade union leader. Before she could take her seat the Act was amended to prohibit any listed communist from being eligible as a Member of Parliament. Subsequently the Africans were deprived of their vote.

What were the factors that made Africans in the Cape vote for members of the Communist Party? They had lost faith in the reformism of liberals and moderates – they wanted representatives who would demand equality. The Communist Party itself, and its members who had in previous years been elected to the Cape Town City Council, had built up an admirable record of fighting for the rights of Africans, of taking up every grievance, of keeping in close touch with the electorate. Mr Kahn's expulsion as their representative was an insult to the African voters and they hit back at the government by choosing representatives each time who belonged to the same militant party as Kahn had done.

The Minister lost no time after the Act was passed in using his powers of banning against the trade unions, more especially against those with mixed memberships, that is African, Coloured and Asian as well as White members. By 1956 seventy-five leading trade union officials had been ordered to resign from their organizations. The government then proceeded with its plan to compel the trade unions to split on racial lines.

Until 1956, when a new Industrial Conciliation Act was passed, White, Coloured and Asian workers could be members of the same Union, and be elected to its executive committee. After January 1957 no new Union would be registered if it had White, Coloured and Asian members. Unions that had been registered before this date would have to restrict their membership to one race, or, alternatively, form separate branches for members of different racial groups and elect an all-White executive. No African unions would receive registration. In 1956 there were 182 registered unions, 113 of which had open memberships.[4]

During the 1950s banning orders increased each year in number, and, with each amendment to the Act, in severity. But they were not accepted without being challenged in the courts.

One of the first to receive an order prohibiting him from attending gatherings was Mr Johnson Ngwevela, of Langa, Cape. Subsequent to his being issued with this order he attended a meeting called to protest against discriminatory laws. He was charged, tried and convicted in the magistrate's court. The Supreme Court dismissed his appeal, the Appeal Court in Bloemfontein upheld it on the grounds that before the Minister could exercise his powers under the Suppression of Communism Act, 1950, to prohibit a person from attending gatherings, the person concerned should be notified, and given an opportunity to show why the order should not be issued. No such opportunity had been given to Mr Ngwevela. The Appeal Court added that the principle of *audi alteram partem* should apply unless Parliament had made clear that it should not.

As a result of Ngwevela's case, all banning orders on listed persons were revoked, cancelled and annulled on 1 May 1954. But the Act was immediately amended making it unnecessary for the

4. Alexander and Simons, 1959, p. 23.

Minister to give listed persons an opportunity of making representations in their defence, or to give all reasons for his actions.[5] Banning orders were reimposed under the amended Act on 29 May
1954.

If requested to do so, the Minister shall give as much of the information that led him to impose the ban as can be disclosed 'without detriment to public policy'. He decides what is in the interests
of 'public policy', and he rarely gives reasons. But a few banned
persons have been given the 'reasons' for their bans, and these
were published in the press. They can be summarized as (a) these
people had attended meetings, carried placards or associated with
organizations that protested against government legislation or
government policy; (b) the Minister was satisfied that if they continued to attend meetings, carry placards and associate with
organizations that opposed the government then the achievement
of communism would be furthered, hence the ban; (c) he could
not disclose the other information he had about these people
without detriment to public policy. It can be pointed out that the
attendance at meetings, the carrying of posters, and the association
with certain organizations were all legal activities.

Mr Kahn, himself a lawyer, was served with banning orders prohibiting him from attending gatherings on 8 July 1954. On the
10th he attended a party. He was charged, tried, convicted in the
magistrate's court. The Supreme Court dismissed his appeal, the
Appeal Court in Bloemfontein upheld it. It ruled that a party was
a purely 'social' gathering. Subsequently the Act was amended to
include social gatherings.

The above are only two of the many appeals lodged against convictions under the Act. They were successful, but frequently the
courts have interpreted the Act to the disadvantage of the individual concerned. Countless hours have been spent by learned
judges in deciding whether playing a game of snooker with a friend
was a gathering. It was. They ruled that joining two friends for a
picnic lunch was a gathering, that sitting in a car a distance away
from where a trade union meeting was being held was attending a
gathering. An elderly African was convicted under the Act for

5. The Riotous Assemblies and Suppression of Communism Amendment Act,
1954, No. 15 of 1954.

failure to notify the police of her change of address: the super-
intendent of the African Township had moved her from one house
to another.

These are all trivial offences and could not possibly be construed as threatening the security of the state. But it is the function
of the Special Branch police to harass and intimidate as well as to
uphold law and order. They bring the charges, and the courts
uphold them.

But in spite of the outlawing of the Communist Party, the removal of trade union officials, police raids, prosecutions of leaders
and banning orders on individuals, the opposition to government
policies continued. When one leader was put out of action another
came forward to take his place. The African National Congress and
the South African Indian Congress were able to organize the De-
fiance of Unjust Laws Campaign in which 8,000 supporters were
prepared to break one or another discriminatory law. Thousands
were prosecuted and went to jail, including the late Patrick
Duncan. The Coloured Peoples' Congress and the Congress of
Democrats (with White members) were formed, and the four congresses convened a mass meeting of 3,000 delegates in Kliptown,
Johannesburg, in 1955. Two years later thousands of workers took
part in a stay-at-home protest called by the congresses and a newly
formed body, the South African Congress of Trade Unions, a
multi-racial federation which accepted the affiliation of any union,
including unregistered Africans' unions. Banning of leaders, and
banning of specific meetings were not enough. In 1960 the
government passed special legislation to enable the State President,
merely by proclamation in the *Government Gazette*, to outlaw
organizations 'with a view to the safety of the public or the maintenance of law and order'. The Unlawful Organizations Act (No.
34 of 1960), was placed on the statute-book and immediately afterwards the African National Congress, which had existed for half a
century, and the Pan Africanist Congress, a splinter body, were
banned.

The largest and most important organizations outlawed to date
are:

The Communist Party – banned in 1950
The African National Congress – banned in 1960

The Pan Africanist Congress – banned in 1960

The Congress of Democrats – banned in 1962

The Spear of the Nation (an offshoot of the A.N.C.) – banned in 1963

Poqo (an offshoot of the Pan Africanist Congress) – banned in 1963

The Defence and Aid Fund – banned in 1966

The Defence and Aid Fund was an organization formed to provide legal defence for political prisoners and financial support for their families.

The 800 individuals who have been banned have been served with orders similar in most respects to the one we reproduce below. There are variations according to the particular circumstances of the individual and we deal with these in a subsequent paragraph.

The particular order hereunder was served on an African in a rural area. But the man on whom they served it is no peasant, accustomed to country life. (Had he been a peasant his banning would have been no less unjust, but might have been somewhat more bearable.) He is a city man, well-educated, an enthusiastic organizer, a man of sociable character. His busy, active life in the city came to an abrupt end – he is confined to his father's kraal, a collection of huts in an African reserve. The nearest town is sixty miles away, the nearest shop two and a half miles away. Both are out of bounds, for the order restricts him to a radius of one mile from his hut. He is deprived of any form of intellectual stimulus, of contact with any human being except his immediate family. He can neither carry on a political discussion, nor chat about the weather with any visitor or passer-by. A potential leader in any free society, he now has no role to play. He has no money with which to buy books or papers, his letters are scrutinized by the police. He has no employment, nor any opportunity of obtaining it.

COPIES OF TWO BANNING ORDERS SERVED ON
AN AFRICAN IN A RURAL AREA

1. Whereas your name appears on the list in the custody of the officer referred to in section *eight* of the Suppression of Communism Act,

1950 (Act No. 44 of 1950), I, Balthazar Johannes Vorster, Minister of Justice in the Republic of South Africa, in terms of paragraph (3) of sub-section (1), section *five* of the said Suppression of Communism Act, 1950, hereby require you for a period commencing on the date on which this notice is delivered to you or tendered to you and expiring on the . . . day of . . ., 1968, not to attend within the Republic of South Africa or the Territory of South West Africa:

(1) any gathering as contemplated in sub-paragraph (i) of the said paragraph (*e*); or

(2) any gathering as contemplated in sub-paragraph (ii) of the said paragraph (*e*) (not being a gathering as is contemplated in the said sub-paragraph (i)) of the nature, class or kind set out below –

    (*a*) any social gathering, that is to say, any gathering at which the persons present also have social intercourse with one another;

    (*b*) any political gathering, that is to say, any gathering at which any form of State or any principle or policy of the government of a State is propagated, defended, attacked, criticized or discussed.

Given under my hand at . . . on this . . .th day of . . ., 1963.

Note: The Magistrate, . . . has in terms of section *five* (1) (*e*) of the above-mentioned Act been empowered to authorize exemptions to the prohibitions contained in this notice.

2. Whereas your name appears on the list in the custody of the officer referred to in section *eight* of the Suppression of Communism Act, 1950, (Act No. 44 of 1950) I, Balthazar Johannes Vorster, Minister of Justice in the Republic of South Africa, hereby in terms of paragraph (*a*) of sub-section (1) of section *ten* of the said Suppression of Communism Act, 1950, prohibit you for a period commencing on the date on which this notice is delivered or tendered to you and expiring on the . . . day of . . . 1968, from –

    (*a*) absenting yourself from the kraal of your father, . . . (which shall for the purposes of this notice be deemed to be the area within a radius of one mile from the most western hut of the said kraal as it is on the date on which this notice is delivered or tendered to you) in the . . . Bantu Reserve in the Magisterial area of . . .

    (*b*) communicating in any manner whatsoever with any person other than –

        (i) a medical practitioner for medical attendance on you or members of your household, if the name of such medical practitioner does not appear on any list in the custody of the officer referred to in section *eight* of the said Suppression of Communism Act, 1950, and no prohibition under the Suppression of Communism Act, 1950, or the Riotous Assemblies Act, 1956, is in force in respect of such Medical Practitioner;

(ii) your wife,

(iii) your children,

(iv) your father,

(v) your sister,

(vi) your brother.

(c) performing any of the following acts, that is to say,

(i) preparing, compiling, printing, publishing or disseminating in any manner whatsoever any publication as defined in section *one* of the Suppression of Communism Act, 1950; or

(ii) participating, or assisting in any manner whatsoever in the preparation, compilation, printing, publication or dissemination of any publication as so defined;

(iii) contributing, preparing or compiling in any manner whatsoever any matter for publication in any publication so defined;

(iv) assisting in any manner whatsoever in the preparation or compiling of any matter for publication in any publication so defined;

(d) Receiving at the said kraal, any visitor other than a medical practitioner for medical attendance on you or members of your family, if the name of such medical practitioner does not appear on any list in the custody of the officer referred to in section *eight* of the said Suppression of Communism Act, 1950, and no prohibition under the Suppression of Communism Act, 1950, or the Riotous Assemblies Act, 1956, is in force in respect of such medical practitioner.

Given under my hand at ... on this ...th day of ... 1963.

Sgd. Minister of Justice.

Notes: The Magistrate, ... has in terms of section *ten* (1) (a) of Act No. 44 of 1950 been empowered to authorize exceptions to the prohibitions contained in this notice.

Your attention is invited to Government Notices Nos. R2130 and R296 dated the 28th December, 1962 and the 22nd February, 1963 respectively.

The texts of Government Notices Nos. R2130 and R296 are printed at the end of this paper.

The Riotous Assemblies Act, 1956 (Act No. 17 of 1956), referred to in the banning order gave the Minister power to prohibit a particular person from attending a particular meeting, or to prohibit the holding of the meeting itself if he had reason to apprehend that feelings of hostility would be engendered between Europeans and non-Europeans by the attendance of such person, or by the holding of such meeting.

It is customary on these types of banning orders to empower the magistrate to authorize exceptions: for example, the person under 'house arrest' might have to undergo an operation for the sake of his health, and the magistrate could then give him written permission to leave his house in order to enter hospital. He might want to attend the funeral of a close relative, and apply to the magistrate for permission to be exempted from the clause prohibiting him from attending gatherings, for this purpose. But exceptions to the prohibitions are not easily obtained, and although the magistrate is given the authority to grant them he does so only on the recommendation of the Special Branch police.

It is the Special Branch, or the Security Police who, in the first place, recommend to the Minister that a certain person should be banned. They recommend whether his banning order should lapse on its expiry date, or be reimposed. They deliver the order personally and read it out to the person concerned, asking him to receipt it. The banned person is under their constant surveillance. They may work through informers. The informer may be a neighbour of the banned person who has been persuaded to report to the Security Police his movements, who visits his home, etc. When it is alleged that South Africa is a 'police state', it does not mean that there is a uniformed policeman at every street corner; it means that the Security Police have power over a man's life, his movements, his activities, his associates, his utterances – all are controlled by them.

Banning orders issued today are more stringent than they were in 1952. Many are now for five years' duration; formerly they were for two. When they expire new orders are frequently issued. They do not take the form of a personal letter from the Minister of Justice, but are roneoed, the name of the person, the particular magisterial district to which he is confined, the particular time and day of the week on which he must report to the police, being entered in spaces which have been left blank. They are signed by the Minister.

There are relatively minor variations to suit the particular circumstances of each person. For example, there is a clause in the orders served on former trade union organizers prohibiting them from being on factory premises, thus precluding them from carrying on with their work. This may not appear on an order served on an African in a rural area. Most prohibitions, such as that on attending meetings, appear on every one. For the aim is the same in every case – the complete isolation of the banned individual from society, the same as it is in respect of those in prison. His isolation is effected in the following manner:

Orders to restrict his movements. (Suppression of Communism Act as amended.[6] Section *ten* and *ten quat*). Either he is restricted to his house, 'house arrest', in which case the Security Police check up at any time of day or night to see that he is there, or he is restricted to his magisterial area, the African township in which he lives, or even to a city block. In such cases he must report to the police at specified times, usually once a week. In times of threatened 'unrest' it is easy for the police to round up all banned people for they know where they are to be found.

Orders to prevent his influencing others by direct, personal contact. (Sections *five* and *nine*.) He is prohibited from attending any gathering where people come together for a common purpose. Gatherings are specified, social, political, educational. Thus having a couple of friends in to dinner is a gathering, standing in a bus queue is not. Attending a church service is a gathering. In 1967 Mrs Helen Joseph obtained permission to attend service during specified hours on Sunday mornings, Mr Eliot Mngadi, former National Treasurer of the Liberal Party was refused.[7] Mr Justice Beyers commented on the 'absurdities of the Act' when he ruled that a mathematics class at the technical college was a 'gathering' in the terms of the Act. Mr O. Dudley, a teacher at Livingstone High School, was thus prohibited from attending.[8]

6. There have been numerous Amending Acts, which, for the sake of space, are not given in detail in this paper.

7. For reports of these cases see *Cape Times*, 7 July 1964, 9 June 1962 and 4 May 1965.

8. ibid.

Mr Terence Beard, a lecturer, was convicted and sentenced to a year's imprisonment, suspended for three years, for breaking his ban. He had sat in the kitchen of Professor Oosthuizen's house while a party was being held in the lounge and dining-room.[9]

The order prohibits a banned person from being in court, unless in the capacity of a witness. This may be in order to prevent demonstrations which were in the past organized to protest when political prisoners were being tried. The order prohibits the banned person from being on the premises of any university, college, or educational institution, or from giving educational instruction to any but his own children. Finally, he is prohibited from being on the premises of any factory, harbour, railway-shed or mine.

Orders to separate him from contact with other races. Orders served on Whites prohibit them from being in any African township, compound, reserve ('Bantu Homeland') or from any area set aside in terms of the Group Areas Act for the residence of Coloured or Asians. Banned Africans are usually restricted to the African Township in which they live and would therefore have little opportunity of contact with Whites other than the police and government officials.

Orders to prohibit him from influencing others by indirect contact, i.e. publications. A publication is defined to include books, pamphlets, posters, placards, drawings, photographs, records. He may not be on the premises of any place where publications are prepared, compiled or printed, nor may he himself assist in the preparation, compilation or printing of any publication. The General Laws Amendment Act, 1962, made it a criminal offence for anyone to publish, record, reproduce by mechanical means, print or disseminate any statement or writing by any person prohibited under sections *five* or *nine* of the Suppression of Communism Act, 1950, from attending gatherings.

What South Africans may or may not read is subject to a great measure of government control. Mr Hepple, in his little book on the subject,[10] enumerates twenty-one laws providing for censorship of one kind or another. It has been calculated that more than

9. ibid.
10. Hepple, 1960.

Ten thousand books and journals were banned under the Customs Act, 1955 (replaced by Act 91 of 1964), and the Entertainments (Censorship) Act of 1931 (replaced by the Publications and Entertainments Act 26 of 1963) between 1956 and 1966. They include all publications from communist countries, publications of the World Federation of Trade Unions, the World Council of Peace, many publications on Africa, and many on South Africa if they criticize apartheid. But it is appropriate in this article to deal only with the powers of banning under the Suppression of Communism Act, 1950.

Section *six* empowers the State President to prohibit the printing, publication or dissemination of any publication if he is satisfied that its purpose is calculated to further the aims of communism or if it is issued by any organization declared to be unlawful. Any person convicted of publishing, printing or disseminating such publication is liable to a term of imprisonment of up to ten years. An amendment stipulated a minimum of three years.

Powers under this Act were first used to ban the *Guardian*, a left-wing newspaper issued weekly for nearly thirty years. No proof that it advocated communism was necessary. The fact that it had consistently opposed White supremacy, exposed the injustices of discriminatory laws, and stood for equality for all was sufficient 'reason'. The same editorial staff overcame the ban by bringing out a new paper, the *Clarion*, to be followed by *Advance* and *New Age* as each was banned in turn. In February 1963, however, each member of the editorial staff was served with an order prohibiting him from entering any premises where publications were prepared, and this made it impossible for them to continue. *Contact*, the monthly journal of the Liberal Party, was not banned but its production made extremely difficult by police raids, seizure of copies, prosecution of the editors, and bannings served on its staff.

Perhaps the most devastating ban on literature is that contained in the amendment to the Suppression of Communism Act, 1950 (Act No. 76 of 1962), making it an offence to publish, print or reproduce any speech, utterance, writing or statement or extract from such speech etc., having been made at any time by any banned person. South Africans can never read Chief Luthuli's call for a peaceful political change, Nelson Mandela's brilliant address to the court prior to his being sentenced to life imprisonment or Mbeki's vivid description of the Pondos' revolt in 1960. While the rest of the world can learn from the scientific papers of eminent South African professors, their own students are kept in ignorance because their writings have been banned.

Orders to prohibit him from influencing organizations. He may not take part in the affairs of any organization specified in his banning order, nor any organization covered by Government Notices Nos. R2130 and R296 of 28 December 1962 and 22 February 1963 (see Annexure 1). Nor may he assist with any publication issued by such organizations.

All recent banning orders contain a prohibition from communicating in any way whatsoever (directly by speaking, indirectly by writing to, or sending messages through a third party) with another banned person. This prohibition is for some the harshest of all. A banned person's closest friends are often other banned people. They have shared common political interests, worked together, attended meetings together, possibly been in jail together. Such friendships are terminated overnight. To receive a banning order is like a bereavement, a shattering experience necessitating a completely new and lonely way of life, and the victim longs for friends to rally round. But there is only silence: banned friends cannot communicate, and those not banned are afraid of being found guilty by association.

This fear is not unfounded. For example, the Minister gave as one of his reasons for renewing Mrs Joseph's ban the fact that she was seen arriving in Cape Town accompanied by Mr M., who was a 'listed communist'. He has more than once implied that those who associate with communists or banned persons are themselves communists, communist-supporters, fellow-travellers, liberalists, etc. He requires no proof. Consequently if one is seen to frequent the home of a banned person, and the home is watched, then the Special Branch take it for granted that one thinks as the banned person does, sympathizes with him, and probably carries on the activities that he is prohibited from performing. Just as people who visit one with an infectious disease run the risk of catching it themselves, so do those who associate with a banned person run the risk of being banned themselves. It is not surprising that they hesitate to visit.

Banning brings economic hardship. Few Africans hold skilled jobs due to lack of training facilities and 'job reservation'. To be prohibited from work in factories – and a factory includes a garage and a building site – or on the railways or docks leaves them with almost no opportunity for employment. Many Coloured and Asian professional men have been hard hit. A Coloured teacher with a B.A. degree is earning 2s. an hour working on the roads for the municipality.[11] Mr B. Kies, a Coloured advocate, was prohibited from defending his client charged with rape because the case was to be heard outside Mr Kies' area of restriction.

The Suppression of Communism Act, 1950, was amended in 1967 to provide that no lawyer may be admitted to the Supreme Court to practise unless he satisfies the Court that his name is not on the list in the custody of the liquidator, and that he has never been convicted of advocating communism, or been a member of an unlawful organization. On an application made by the Secretary of Justice, the Supreme Court must order the name of any listed person or person convicted of advocating communism to be struck off the roll.

Mr Lewis Baker, convicted in 1965 on charges under the Suppression of Communism Act, 1950, was struck off the roll in November 1967. Mr J. N. Singh and Mr I. C. Meer, both attorneys living in Durban, were struck off shortly afterwards. Both had been banned, and were former vice-presidents of the Natal Indian Congress. They had been in practice for twenty years, and will find it almost impossible to obtain other employment.[12] Those charged in future with political offences whom Singh and Meer would have been willing to defend, being sympathetic and unafraid, will also be the sufferers.

Individuals react to their banning orders in different ways. Mr Yusuf Nagdee was found hanged at his home in Johannesburg in August 1965, shortly after he had been restricted. His family said that he had been depressed since his ban especially as he had had to give up his job as a commercial traveller. A few of the banned

11. *Cape Times*, 28 September 1966.
12. *Sunday Times*, 12 November 1967.

have, under pressure, sought relief by making their peace with the Security Police and having their orders withdrawn. In the case of Mr Ndamse, former lecturer at Fort Hare, representations from Chief Kaiser Matanzima, to whom he was a close adviser, succeeded in obtaining the withdrawal of his ban. Matanzima wanted his services for the Transkei Department of Bantu Education. Few have openly defied the ban and exchanged their restrictions for imprisonment.

Many, mostly White and Coloured, have escaped from their bans by leaving South Africa on exit permits. Such permits are granted by the Minister on condition that the banned person does not return to his home country. Some felt that to stay in South Africa and comply with the restrictions was to succumb to government pressure. Others simply wanted to lead a normal life in a free country, especially for the sake of their children. For children, too, have suffered on account of their parents' bannings.

A few dedicated people, banned, or knowing that they could not long avoid a ban, escaped from the country to carry on the struggle in other parts of Africa, even if this might mean paying with their lives for the liberation of their people. But the great majority of banned Africans are prepared to stay and endure their hardships – silenced by force, hearts and minds unconquered.

What has been the reaction of the South African community as a whole? At first there was an outcry against the injustice of depriving a man of his liberty when he was guilty of no crime. Even today, bans on important people like Dr Hoffenberg of the Cape Town Medical School cause a stir. But bans on less well-known people are no longer press news. Protests, demonstrations, deputations to those in authority, letters to the press have died down. It would appear from the names of Africans reported as banned in the government gazettes that many prisoners who had been convicted of political crimes are issued with banning orders immediately after their release from jail. They swell the number of the banned, but there have been no protests.

I think the reaction can be explained by examining the reasons for banning orders.

Is banning punitive? This is the generally accepted idea. Even the banned person's closest friends are suspicious that he may have 'done something' to warrant a ban. The question is always asked, 'But what has he done, what could he have done?' Is this the expression of a naïve belief that one does not get punished unless one is guilty? Or perhaps it expresses a hope that he has, in fact, 'done something' to offend the authorities, for then one can escape such a fate oneself by being careful to do nothing at all?

But the reason is not punitive. It is preventive. Opponents of government policies are usually sincere; if they can, they will continue to oppose and try to get others to do so too. The government is aware of this, and the reason for the ban is to prevent their continued opposition and to intimidate others from following their lead.

Many thousands of good citizens disapprove of the worst excesses of apartheid, but they are much too afraid of being banned to do anything about it.

When the Coloured area called District Six, in Cape Town, was recently declared a White area under the Group Areas Act, it meant that thousands of Coloured families who had lived there all their lives, had their schools, churches, businesses there, would have to move. A small and harmless District Six Defence Committee was formed. It was not to oppose the move, but to find ways of alleviating the hardships it would cause. For example, it would try to get fair prices for the houses the Coloured owners would be forced to sell. Two members of the committee were served with banning orders, four were warned by the Magistrate that they were liable to be banned if they carried on what they were doing. The effect is that others are afraid to come on to the committee.

These warnings are an effective part of the government's policy of intimidation. The Act provides that before making up his mind to issue a ban, the Minister may require a magistrate to give a warning to a certain person to desist from any activities which might further the achievement of communism. There is no way of knowing whether someone has had such a warning unless the person concerned divulges it. But it is known that in addition to the members of the District Six Defence Committee who received warnings, there were seven people in Port Elizabeth, none of whom was listed or banned, who received such magisterial

warnings. They subsequently felt it advisable to resign from every organization to which they belonged in order to lessen their chances of being banned. It can be assumed that the activities about which they were warned were all perfectly legal: if they were not, the persons concerned would have been arrested and charged.

The effect of banning is widespread intimidation of the whole community. Bannings, as well as saracens, contribute to Vorster's 'peaceful' South Africa.

The editor of the *Rand Daily Mail*, Mr Laurence Gander, quoting extensively from *Die Burger*, a Nationalist paper, explains what is in the mind of the Minister when he decides to issue a banning order.[13] Briefly, the argument runs thus. Liberals, humanitarians, egalitarians, as well as communists, believe in an integrated, non-racial South African society: the White electorate has shown clearly that it rejects such an ideal, and only the Whites hold political power in South Africa. Such a society therefore can never be achieved by peaceful, constitutional means. Those who continue to hold out the possibility of this kind of society to the African, Coloured and Asian people are thus encouraging them to achieve it by violent, unconstitutional methods, the only methods available to them. Communists believe in violence to achieve their ends. Therefore liberals, humanitarians, egalitarians are equated with communists in that the activities of all of them must produce similar results; therefore the powers to ban under the Suppression of Communism Act, 1950, may quite logically be used against all alike. There is no need for anyone to have 'done anything', or to have infringed any law. If he opposes the *status quo* he is encouraging others to upset it by violence, hence he must be silenced, rendered inactive, banned.

Mr J. C. Greyling, Nationalist M.P. for Ventersdorp, has put the government's attitude in one sentence. He said: 'The time has come to ban, like communists, anyone who opposes apartheid.'[14]

13. *Rand Daily Mail*, 18 November 1967.
14. *Cape Times*, 15 June 1959.

BIBLIOGRAPHY

Alexander, Ray, and Simons, H. J., *Job Reservation and the Trade Unions*, Enterprise, Cape, 1959.

Bunting, Brian, *The Rise of the South African Reich*, Penguin, 1964.

Carter, Gwendolen, *The Politics of Inequality*, Thames & Hudson, 1958.

Hepple, Alexander, *Censorship and Press Control in South Africa*, published by the author, 1960.

International Defence and Aid Fund, *Information Service*, 1967/8.

Joseph, Helen, *Tomorrow's Sun*, Hutchinson, 1966.

Mbeki, Govan, *The Peasants' Revolt*, Penguin, 1964.

Roux, E. R., *Time Longer than Rope*, Gollancz, 1948.

South African Institute of Race Relations, *Annual Surveys*.

COPIES OF NOTICES RELATING TO THE SUPPRESSION OF COMMUNISM ACT, 1950

DEPARTMENT OF JUSTICE

No. R296   22nd February, 1963

Notice in terms of Section Five Ter *of the Suppression of Communism Act, 1950 (Act No. 44 of 1950)*

By virtue of the powers vested in me by sub-section (1) of section *five ter* of the Suppression of Communism Act, 1950 (Act No. 44 of 1950), I, Balthazar Johannes Vorster, Minister of Justice of the Republic of South Africa, hereby prohibit all persons –

   (*a*) whose names appear on any list in the custody of the officer referred to in section *eight* of the said Act;

   (*b*) who were office-bearers, officers or members of any organization which has under sub-section (2) of section *two* of the said Act been declared to be an unlawful organization; or

   (*c*) in respect of whom any prohibition under the said Act by way of notices, addressed and delivered or tendered to them is in force, and –

    (i) who are not office-bearers, officers or members of an organization which in any manner prepares, compiles, prints, publishes or disseminates any publication as defined in the said Suppression of Communism Act, 1950, or which in any manner participates or assists in the preparation, compilation, printing, publication or dissemination of any such publication, from becoming office-bearers, officers or members of any such organization; or

   (ii) who are office-bearers, officers or members of an organization which in any manner prepares, compiles, prints, publishes or disseminates any publication as defined in the said Suppression of Communism Act, 1950, or which in any manner participates or assists in the preparation, compilation, printing, publication or dissemination of any such publication, from being office-bearers, officers or members of any such organization as from the 1st April, 1963,

unless my written consent thereto, or that of the magistrate concerned has been obtained.

B. J. VORSTER
Minister of Justice

DEPARTMENT OF JUSTICE

No. R2130   28th December 1962

Notice in terms of Section Five Ter *of the Suppression of Communism Act, 1950 (Act No. 44 of 1950)*

By virtue of the powers vested in me by sub-section (1) of section *five ter* of the Suppression of Communism Act, 1950 (Act No. 44 of 1950), I, Balthazar Johannes Vorster, Minister of Justice of the Republic of South Africa, hereby prohibit all persons –

    (*a*) whose names appear on any list in the custody of the officer referred to in section *eight* of the said Act;

    (*b*) who were office-bearers, officers or members of any organization which has under sub-section (2) of section *two* of the said Act been declared to be an unlawful organization; or

    (*c*) in respect of whom any prohibition under the said Act by way of notices addressed and delivered or tendered to them is in force,

and –

    (i) who are not office-bearers, officers or members of an organization referred to in Part I or II of the Annexure to the Notice, from becoming office-bearers, officers or members of any such organization; or

    (ii) who are office-bearers, officers or members of an organization referred to in Part I or II of the said Annexure, from being office-bearers, officers or members of any such organization as from the 1st February, 1963,

unless my written consent thereto, or that of the magistrate concerned has been obtained.

This prohibition shall not apply to a trade union or employers' organization registered as such in terms of the Industrial Conciliation Act, 1956 (Act No. 28 of 1956).

B. J. VORSTER
Minister of Justice

ANNEXURE

Part I (Particular Organizations)

1. African Peoples' Democratic Union of Southern Africa.
2. African Students' Association.
3. African Students' Union of South Africa.
4. African Youth League, also known as Langa Youth League.
5. All-African Convention.
6. Anti-Coloured Affairs Department.
7. Basutoland Congress Party.
8. Bechuanaland People's Party.
9. Cape African Teachers' Association.
10. Cape Peace Council.
11. Civil Rights League.
12. Congress Alliance, also known as Congress Movement or Congress of the People.
13. Federation of South African Women.
14. Modern Youth Society.

15. Natal Indian Congress.
16. Natal Indian Congress Youth League.
17. Natal Peace Council.
18. Non-European Unity Movement.
19. Progressive Forum.
20. Society of Young Africa.
21. South African Coloured Peoples' Congress.
22. South African Congress of Trade Unions.
23. South African Congress of Youth.
24. South African Democratic Union.
25. South African Indian Congress.
26. South African Peace Council.
27. South African Society of Peace and Friendship with the Soviet Union.
28. South-West Africa National Union.
29. South-West Africa Peoples' Organization.
30. Students' Liberal Association.
31. Swaziland Progressive Party.
32. Teachers' League of South Africa.
33. Transvaal Indian Congress.
34. Transvaal Indian Youth Congress.
35. Transvaal Peace Council.
36. Youth Action Committee.

Part II (*organizations of a specified nature, class or kind*)

1. Any organization which is in any manner affiliated to or a subsidiary of any organization mentioned in Part I or which promotes or furthers or performs any act or is engaged in any activity which is calculated to promote or further any of the objects of any such organization or which has as an object the achievement or promotion or furtherance of any object of any such organization.

2. Any organization which in any manner propagates, defends, attacks, criticizes or discusses any form of State or any principle or policy of the Government of a State, or which in any manner undermines the authority of the Government of a State.

3. Any trade union or employers' organization as defined hereunder, viz. –

'trade union' means any number of employees in any particular undertaking, industry, trade or occupation associated together primarily for the purpose of regulating relations in that undertaking, industry, trade or occupation between themselves or some of them and their employers or some of their employers;

'employers' organization' means any number of employers in any particular undertaking, industry, trade or occupation associated together primarily for the purpose of regulating relations in that undertaking, industry, trade or occupation between themselves or some of them and their employees or some of their employees.

The Soviet Treatment of Dissenters and the Growth of a Civil Rights Movement

Peter Reddaway

We have seen that in South Africa banning can turn persons into 'non-persons'. In the Soviet Union, as Mr Reddaway shows, similar results are achieved, but by very different means. Forced labour and such devices as confinement to a mental hospital take the place of banning and house arrest.

Partly this may be because the number of known 'deviants' in the Soviet Union is greater than in South Africa. It may also be that in the Soviet Union there is not the same residual concern for human rights as may sometimes be discerned in South Africa. At the same time, political misfits in the Soviet Union may be tortured and starved, but are relatively seldom executed, whereas thirty years ago they would simply have been shot.

Thus the Soviet Union is no longer totally cut off from the world. There is a far greater flow of information than in recent years, as is shown by the very fact that Mr Reddaway has been able to obtain the documents (a very small selection of those in his possession) which are printed after his paper. The Soviet Government is no longer totally impervious to world opinion and internally there are sufficient stirrings to support Mr Reddaway's contention that a civil rights movement is coming to birth. The progress is perhaps not great, but it is there. –C.R.H.

We consider it our duty to draw attention to the fact that there are in the prisons and camps several thousands of political prisoners, about whom almost no one knows. They are held in inhuman conditions of compulsory labour, on a semi-starvation diet, abandoned to the arbitrary actions of the administration.

[From the letter of February 1968 to the Presidium of the Consultative Meeting of Communist Parties in Budapest from twelve Soviet citizens, including Larisa Daniel (b. *c.* 1928) and Dr Pavel Litvinov (b. 1937) – see Document 1.]

I don't know whether now, in the sixties, there exist anywhere on earth outside our country such conditions for political prisoners: legalized lawlessness plus legalized hunger plus legalized forced labour. I am convinced of one thing: that such conditions can persist in our country only because no one knows about them, apart from their organizers and perpetrators. If the public were informed of the actual conditions how could you protest about the treatment of political prisoners abroad? So far only our political prisoners are able, when they read these protests of yours in the papers, to assess the monstrous ambiguity of the situation, the extreme contradiction between propaganda 'for export' and practice at home.

[From the open letter by Anatolii Marchenko (b. 1939) to leading Soviet figures, April 1968 – see Document 2.]

Not less than 10–15 million Soviet people perished from torture and execution in the prisons of the N.K.V.D., in the camps for exiled kulaks and so-called 'sub-kulaks' and members of their families, in the camps 'with no right of correspondence' (these were in fact the forerunners of the Nazi death camps; there existed, for example, the practice of mass machine-gunnings of thousands of prisoners on account of the 'overcrowdedness' of the camps or on the receipt of 'special orders'), in the coal mines of Norilsk and Vorkuta from cold, starvation and the crushing labour . . . during the deportation of whole peoples – the Crimean Tatars, the Volga Germans, the Kalmyks and many other peoples . . .

In conclusion I summarize certain concrete suggestions. . . . 4. It is essential to abolish all the anti-constitutional laws and instructions which violate human rights. 5. It is essential to amnesty the political prisoners . . . and immediately to improve the camp conditions of political prisoners.

[From the essay 'Reflections on Progress, Peaceful Coexistence and Intellectual Freedom' by a leading nuclear scientist, Academician A. D. Sakharov (b. 1921), June 1968.]

THESE passages indicate the main features of a still inadequately documented subject: (a) Soviet dissenters continue today to receive inhuman treatment; (b) neither Soviet nor world public opinion has any real conception of the size of the problem; (c) its size is not in fact very surprising if one looks coolly at the relevant political and legal facts of the recent past and the present; (d) this is what various groups of Soviet citizens have begun to do, thus giving rise to the early stages of a potentially very powerful civil rights movement; (e) the latter's potential strength is suggested by the fearlessness with which almost all the signatories of protest documents authenticate them with their full name and address, despite the severe risks involved.

This essay aims only to outline the subject, flavour being added by the selected documents (pp. 100–120). It merely gives some idea of scope and main issues, perhaps indicating where more detailed research is most needed.

HISTORICAL BACKGROUND

Political freedom, even in the period after 1905, was never very extensive in tsarist Russia. Political offenders were usually exiled, and only sometimes either made to do physical labour or – and this could prove fatal – incarcerated in the Shlisselburg or the Peter-Paul fortress. But they never totalled more than a few thousand. That the situation in this respect deteriorated under Stalin to the extent indicated by Academician Sakharov – and many more millions, besides the 'not less than 10–15 million' who perished, experienced the camps and survived – is no revelation to those who have read the painstaking research of scholars like Dallin, Nicolaevsky and Barton on the Stalin period and later,[1] as well as many memoirs by ex-prisoners both Soviet – like Alexander Solzhenitsyn, General Gorbatov and Evgenia Ginzburg – and non-Soviet.[2] But a surprising number of non-Soviet specialists on Soviet affairs appear not to have done this, and naturally Soviet

1. D. J. Dallin and B. I. Nicolaevsky, *Forced Labor in Soviet Russia*, Yale U.P., New Haven, 1947; Paul Barton, *L'Institution concentrationnaire en Russie (1930–1957)*, Plon, Paris, 1959, and 'An End to Concentration Camps?' in *Problems of Communism*, Washington D.C., XI, No. 2, March-April 1962, pp. 38–46; see also United Nations, *Report of the 'ad hoc' Committee on Forced Labour*, Geneva, 1953; S. Wolin and R. M. Slusser (eds), *The Soviet Secret Police*, Methuen, 1957; and D. J. Dallin's chapter 'Forced Labor' in his *The Changing World of Soviet Russia*, Yale U.P., New Haven, 1956, pp. 127–68.

2. Robert Conquest has now performed the enormous task of collating all this material with that listed in note 1 and presenting the results in concise and lucid form. His careful calculations produce a figure of about 20,000,000 deaths at the hands of the N.K.V.D. between 1930 and 1953 (thus roughly coinciding with Sakharov's estimate, which omits the Great Famine victims). See his *The Great Terror: Stalin's Purge of the Thirties*, Macmillan, 1968, pp. 332–66, 494, 509–16, 525–35.

citizens have had little chance either to profit from this research or freely to conduct their own. Hence the widespread non-Soviet ignorance on the subject and also the absence until recently of Soviet documents such as those quoted above – factors which have in certain ways reinforced each other.

Today, however, in the words of Sakharov,[3] 'our country has started along the path of cleansing itself from the filth of stalinism. In Chekhov's phrase "drop by drop we are squeezing the slave out of ourselves", learning to express our own views, not glancing over our shoulders at the boss and not fearing for our own lives.' Admittedly, he finds this process severely impeded by neo-stalinists in the key positions of power, as does the well-known Soviet writer Lydia Chukovskaya, who in an open letter of February 1968[4] put her finger on the mainspring of neo-stalinism. As she wrote, certificates of innocence have been given to those prisoners of Stalin

who have been lucky enough to survive. Excellent. They have returned. But where are those who were the cause of it all? Those who faked the charges against millions of people? ... Those who gave the orders for those who were sentenced to be blackened in the press? Who are these people, where are they and what are they doing today? Who, when, and where has counted their crimes, committed in comfort, methodically, peacefully – day in day out, year in year out?

They are in fact, she writes, in comfortable jobs or on big pensions, while no national day, no monuments, commemorate their innocent victims: 'No, it is not a question of revenge, I do not suggest tooth for tooth. Vengeance does not attract me. I'm talking not about a criminal court but a social one. Because although the informers, the hangmen and the provocateurs have well deserved execution, our people have not deserved the horror of being fed on executions.' Lines such as these perhaps especially help non-Soviet readers to get inside a psychological situation far outside

3. For full Russian text see the booklet A. D. Sakharov, *Razmyshleniya o progresse, mirnom sosushchestvovanii i intellektual'noi svobode*, Possev Verlag, Frankfurt, translated as *Progress, Coexistence and Intellectual Freedom*, André Deutsch, 1968, with notes by Harrison Salisbury.

4. Entitled *Ne kazn', no mysl', no slovo, Possev*, Frankfurt, No. 8, 1968, pp. 47–9, translated in *Problems of Communism*, XVII, 5, 1968.

their personal experience, and they throw into sharper relief the courage of the writers of documents such as those quoted here. This courage is particularly great as all the documents come from the post-Krushchev period, which has seen a steady process of re-stalinization and the reactivation of many stalinists.

THE PRISONS AND THE CAMPS

As Documents 2 and 3 show at length, a great deal is known about conditions in the Dubrovlag (or Potma) complex of camps in Mordovia, 200 miles south-east of Moscow. This information can be checked and re-checked against further highly detailed accounts by S. Y. Karanvansky (b. 1920) and an anonymous prisoner, published in a remarkable new book about the treatment of Ukrainian political prisoners, *The Chornovil Papers*,[5] as well as against other such accounts by the historian Valentyn Moroz (b. 1936) and the lawyer Ivan Kandyba (b. 1930), and many related materials in a forthcoming book.[6] More recently still, in June 1968, Sakharov added a few details:

At the present time the majority of political prisoners are held in the Dubrovlag group of camps on the territory of Mordovia (together with the criminal prisoners it holds about 30,000 prisoners in all). According to available information, beginning in 1961 the régime in these camps

---

5. By Vyacheslav Chornovil, with an introduction by Frederick Barghoorn, McGraw-Hill, Maidenhead, Berks, 1968. See pp. 210–13, 218–19, 91–7. Hereafter referred to as *Chornovil*. Chornovil (b. 1937) is a journalist who put together this collection of materials, many of them written in or relating to Potma, from and about twenty of the Ukrainian intellectuals arrested in 1965. It was taken abroad and in November 1967 he received an eighteen-month sentence. The original Ukrainian (and a few Russian) texts of most of *Chornovil* are in V. Chornovil (ed.), *Lykho z rozumu – portrety dvadtsyaty 'zlochyntsiv'*, P.I.U.F., 3, rue du Sabot, Paris, 1967. This contains portraits of most of the prisoners and (p. 296) a map of Mordovia.

6. Michael Browne (ed.), *Ferment in the Ukraine*, Macmillan, 1969. Moroz's brilliant essay, providing a deep insight into the psychology of the degraded people who administer Potma, is already available in abridged form in *Problems of Communism*, Washington D.C., XVII, 4, 1968, pp. 84–90. Further information on Potma should become available in 1970, when the British lecturer Gerald Brooke finishes serving a five-year sentence there for spreading anti-Soviet leaflets. In 1966 he was deliberately starved by the administration and shown to his wife in emaciated condition in an attempt to blackmail the British Government into exchanging him for two Soviet spies imprisoned in Britain.

became steadily more cruel, and an ever greater role was played by the camp personnel remaining from Stalin's time. (In fairness it should be noted that very recently a certain improvement has been noticed.[7] One may hope that this change will prove permanent).

The most detailed account of contemporary camp and prison conditions about which we know is clearly the unpublished book by Anatolii Marchenko, 'My Testimony', mentioned in Document 2, which has reached the West but not been available to the author. Document 2, in fact, appears to be a summary of parts of the book and is basic reading for a clear understanding of this chapter. It should at once be noted that Marchenko, like the author of Document 3, Larisa Daniel, and also the authors of documents in *Chornovil*, deals only with the camps in Potma which are of 'strict' (*strogii*) or 'special' (*osobyi*) régime. These are the two toughest of the four main types, the others being 'ordinary' (*obshchii*) and 'hard' (*usilennyi*).

As many of the documents stress, the most disturbing aspect of the 'strict' camps, the least severe variety to which political prisoners are sent, is the dietary norm of 2,400 calories a day, since very few chances exist of buying extra food. Indeed after studying the details in Marchenko's documents a consultant dietician of Amnesty reported that (*a*) the daily menu described seemed in fact to amount to only just over 2,000 calories and was also very unbalanced, lacking, for example, vitamin C, and (*b*) men doing manual labour such as that at Potma in fact need about 4,000 to keep fit. The 'norm' of 2,400 was below even the 2,500 needed by a sedentary, elderly man. As for the 1,300 calories per day of the 'special' régime, this was enough only for a young child and would quickly result in severe illness.

---

7. Sakharov may here be reflecting the improvements reported to have been introduced as a result of a hunger strike in Camp 17 in February 1968, in which the writers Yulii Daniel, Boris Zdorovets, Viktor Kalnynsh, Sergei Moshkov, Valerii Ronkin and Yuri Shukhevych took part. The improvements involved promises of greater Procuracy control over the administration's actions. It is extremely interesting to note that Daniel is a Moscow intellectual, Moshkov and Ronkin Leningrad intellectuals, Zdorovets a Baptist, and Shukhevych a Ukrainian 'bourgeois nationalist', while Kalnynsh (a Latvian name) may well be another 'bourgeois nationalist'. All this suggests a demonstrative alliance in the camp between representatives of the country's most prominent dissident groups. For more details on Shukhevych, see *Chornovil*, pp. 208–9.

Thus one can only suppose with the document writers that the authorities deliberately set such low norms in the hope that prisoners will either become submissive and publicly denounce their own views, actions and friends, or die through illness or some desperate act brought on by permanent weakness. With justification Karavansky pointed his finger in 1966 at U.S.S.R. Procurator-General Rudenko who, though responsible for the maintenance of legality,

did not protest against the introduction of dreadful starvation conditions into the U.S.S.R. camp system. Having acted in 1945 as state prosecutor at the Nuremberg trials Rudenko knows only too well what crimes against humanity are. Yet he quite knowingly persists in sanctioning the cannibalistic rules of the camp régime for prisoners, which were drawn up by the Ministries for the Preservation of Public Order of the union republics. The application of these rules to political prisoners can only be regarded as a crime against humanity.[8]

About the 'special' régime camps, not much discussed by Marchenko, Karavansky writes:

People are locked up for decades in concrete cells, without windows. ... Deprived of air and light, emaciated by the starvation ration, and stuffed seven or ten men to a narrow, stuffy cell, the people little by little lose their resemblance to human beings. There are frequent cases of suicide (for instance, the prisoner Susey), mutilation and insanity. Prisoners open their veins and write in blood on the walls 'Death to Svyatkin'. (Svyatkin is the K.G.B. official for camp No. 10). One prisoner cut off his ears, placed them in a parcel, and addressed it to the Twenty-Second Party Congress. Driven to despair, they tattoo on their foreheads the words 'Slave of the C.P.S.U.' (Communist Party of the Soviet Union). This act is as severely punished as sabotage, subversion or calling for the overthrow of the Government, by execution by a firing squad (as with the prisoner Malay). ... Detention in the 'special régime' camps over many years means the absolute physical and moral transformation from human being to animal. ... These camps ... are a shameful left-over of the genocide of prisoners carried out in the camps by Beria, Yezhov and Yagoda.[9]

8. *Chornovil*, p. 219. Karavansky, a writer, was sentenced to twenty-five years in 1945, released in 1960, then rearrested in 1965 to serve out the sentence in Potma. On this arbitrariness of Rudenko's see ibid., pp. 169, 191–6.

9. ibid., p. 213.

Kandyba, after giving details similar to Marchenko's about the normal 'semi-starvation rations' in Potma, 'allegedly comprising 2,300–2,400 calories', distinguishes between a severe ration in the camp prisons of 1,324 calories and a less severe one of 1,937, commenting: 'Those who refuse to work are kept on the 1,324 calories ration.' Reverting to the normal prisoners, he continues,

We are forced to fulfil our work-norm 100%, while the jobs we perform require 3,500–4,000 calories (see the journal *Zdorov'e* [Health], No. 9, 1966, pp. 26–7). Try to live that way. Under such conditions many suffer from T.B., heart disease and other illnesses. Medical attention is very poor; there is a shortage or complete lack of necessary medicines and their receipt from relatives by parcel post is prohibited.

The human anguish constantly provoked by these conditions, as well as the attitude needed to endure them, show through in a document by another Ukrainian, the poet and teacher Mikhaylo Masyutko (b. 1918). In a letter to his wife from Potma dated October 1966 he writes:

How sorry I felt for you on that cold, rainy day when you were crying at the gate, trying to visit me. How I pitied your tears! I wrote all about it in my letters. But when I realized that my letters hadn't reached you, I started to write more restrained ones in the hope that they would find their way to you. . . . In my job I must pull loads weighing 90 kg. and more. The strain tears apart the fresh scar where I had the operation, so that it is almost impossible for me to cough and to breathe deeply – I have such a sharp pain in my chest. Out here it is not as you think it is; if one is submissive, one can perish. [*Chornovil*, p. 148].

This is only a small sample of all the first-hand material now available on Potma.

As for 'ordinary' and 'hard' régime camps, to which most religious prisoners go (only a few get 'strict' régime), conditions are generally less bad, though not always. Section 6 of Document 4 portrays some of the many hardships of Baptists in such camps. P. S. Overchuk (b. 1932), mentioned here, has himself described life in his 'ordinary' régime camp in the Ukraine,[10] including his spell of ten days in the punishment cell for refusing to stop praying:

10. See *Problems of Communism*, XVII, 4, 1968, pp. 96–7. The document, a petition to the Ukrainian Chief Procurator Glukh, is dated 10 May 1967.

This is a cell without windows, light or air, of 12–14 square metres. Electric light comes from the corridor through a Judas-window with a narrow grille, which is about 15–20 cm. high and the width of the door, 80 cm. Into such a cell, deprived of air and light about twelve to fifteen or more people are crowded, after they have had their warm clothes, handkerchiefs and bedding taken away. In such a cell one can sleep on the wooden floor (a platform), either in a crouching position or sitting.

During the ten days the cell is not opened for airing, and not for a single moment may the prisoners leave the room, not even to attend to natural needs, or for essential hygienic necessities. Food is served in a trough – 450 gm. of black bread, 600–700 gm. of watery soup, and on alternate days a bit of tasteless, cold food with no fat content (the ration for five days is less than one day's food ration for a normal prisoner) . . . After I had been there for eight days a great multitude of lice appeared.

Another document[11] about an 'ordinary' régime camp concerns the alarming case of the Baptist leader G. P. Vins, briefly referred to several times in Document 4. The former document comes from 176 Kiev Baptists, who signed it on behalf of their community of 400, and is dated 25 February 1968. It reports that in the summer of 1967 Vins (b. 1928) was transferred to a camp at Taly, near Kizel in the Urals, and continues:

The Kiev E.C.B. community possesses reliable information about the intention of certain agencies to liquidate Georgi Petrovich Vins through camp conditions. Vins has now been reduced to a state of complete physical exhaustion. Violating the existing regulations of the Ministry of Public Order, which govern the treatment of prisoners in camps, the camp authorities made Vins, a member of the building brigade, walk under guard five to six miles every day to this place of work and back, through rugged, mountainous terrain (ten to twelve miles daily in all). Although by profession an engineer, he was then employed as a manual hauler, dragging logs from the forest for the construction of railway buildings.

Because of all this, Vins in October 1967 contracted an infection from which his body has so far not recovered and which, combined with excessive work, has reduced him to complete exhaustion and made him develop a heart disease. In addition, boils have appeared all

11. See ibid., pp. 101–2, and, for full Russian text, *Possev*, No. 7, 1968, pp. 5–6.

over his arms and body. Sometimes he has fainted at work or on his way there. Nevertheless his serious state of health has not exempted him from work. Eventually he contracted an inguinal hernia owing to the work, which was beyond his strength, but even after this he was still forced to do hard physical labour, although this meant his health would be completely broken and his life endangered . . .

Because of continuous threats from certain quarters to destroy Vins and the obvious intention of carrying them out, we believers, as well as Vins himself and his relatives, distrust any surgical intervention carried out on the camp premises – we have every good reason to hold this view . . .

In addition, on 26 January 1968, the deputy head of the Taly prison group, Major Tesov, instructed the camp commander in the presence of Vins to employ him, an invalid, in exceptionally heavy physical work . . .

Thus while certain model camps exist, and are shown on occasion to foreigners,[12] even ordinary régime camps appear frequently to be the scenes of barbarism.

Turning to the prisons, little is available by way of recent, detailed first-hand accounts, although Amnesty has considerable information on prisons in Minsk and Mogilev in the early 1960s and Greville Wynne has described his prolonged torture and the appalling conditions in Moscow's Lubyanka prison and the Vladimir prison in the same period.[13] (Marchenko not surprisingly brackets the latter prison with the 'special régime' camps.) In 1966 Mykhaylo Horyn (b. 1930), one of the Ukrainian intellectuals, had bad experiences in the Voronezh prison and the 'Kholodna Hora' (Cold Mountain) prison of Kharkov,[14] and in 1964 torture was freely applied, with fatal results, on the Baptist Nikolai Khmara in the Barnaul prison in the Altai.[15] Further, as described briefly

12. See, for example, the illustrated report on a camp for juveniles at Iksha, near Moscow – a modern equivalent of the Bolshevo camp which so impressed Beatrice Webb and others in the 30s – by George Feifer in the *Sunday Times Magazine*, 28 May 1967.

13. See the chapters 'Lubyanka' and 'Vladimir' in G. Wynne, *The Man from Moscow*, Hutchinson, 1967, also the photograph of Wynne on his release, showing his emaciation as compared to his pre-arrest photograph.

14. *Chornovil*, pp. 112–13.

15. See Michael Bourdeaux, *Religious Ferment in Russia: Protestant Opposition to Soviet Religious Policy*, Macmillan, 1968, pp. 79–82. This book gives massive docu-

in Document 4, the Baptist Kovalchuk almost died after inhuman torture during his detention in Rovno and Lvov.[16] On the other hand, Amnesty has a reliable report from the early 1960s about the cleanliness and generally excellent condition of at least one part of the Lefortovo prison in Moscow.

POLICE BRUTALITY OUTSIDE THE PRISONS AND CAMPS

Brutality in this category has been applied – in police stations and public places – especially to those Baptist and Orthodox groups who have resisted some of the more vicious forms of religious persecution and discrimination. The 'underground' literature from these groups available outside the U.S.S.R., much of it relentlessly documenting the new persecution begun in 1958–9, now amounts in all to several hundred thousands words.[17] Document 4 exemplifies the genre, while the following Orthodox account[18] conveys the violent flavour of the anti-religious drive in the northern Ukraine:

---

mentation on the conflict of a section of the Baptists with the state over their demand for greater religious freedom, and reproduces their tabulated data on some 200 Baptist prisoners as of 1964. A list of similar size, but containing mostly different names, appears at the end of the full text of Document 4, recording the situation of 1967. After this paper was finished a new list – of August 1968 – became available, documenting 233 current prisoners and giving for the first time the full addresses of the places of imprisonment of 140 of them. These people were in 88 different camps scattered throughout most of the Soviet Union, 5 of the 88 belonging to the Potma complex. Exact sentences are known for 219 prisoners, and average just over 3 years in length. Of these people 1 is in Vladimir prison, 35 are in strict régime camps, 9 in hard régime camps, 165 in ordinary régime camps, 4 in exile, and 5 have conditional sentences. The list will appear in X. Howard-Johnston and R. Harris (eds.), *Christian Letters from Russia*, Hodder, 1969.

16. Kovalchuk's own lengthy account, dated 31 July 1966 and sent to Mr Brezhnev and others, is in *Religion in Communist-Dominated Areas* (R.C.D.A.), New York, VI, 15–16 August 1967, pp. 127–33, and in Howard-Johnston and Harris, op. cit.

17. See Peter Reddaway, 'Freedom of Worship and the Law' (and accompanying documents) in *Problems of Communism*, XVII, 4, 1968, pp. 21–9, 96–114, for a survey of the sources and the main issues. See also M. Bourdeaux, op.cit., esp. pp. 118–24, and his forthcoming *Patriarch and Prophets: Tensions in the Russian Orthodox Church*, Macmillan, 1969.

18. Extract from a 12,000-word appeal to President Podgorny, written in mid 1966 by the Spiritual Council of the Pochaev Lavra. It summarizes many earlier documents and appeared in *Phoenix 1966*, edited by the young poet and pacifist Yuri Galanskov (b. 1939). Russian text in *Vestnik russkogo studencheskogo khristianskogo dvizheniya*, 84, Paris, 1967, pp. 39–69. English text in Bourdeaux, *Patriarch and Prophets*.

Belik and Gordeev with their squad of militiamen and volunteer police, continued their non-stop efforts to track down worshippers and check up on Christians in Pochaev. On the evening of 12 June 1964 they came to the house of Anastasia Religa, made a search and found Marfa in the attic. Belik gave orders to deal out such maltreatment that she would never again want to worship in Pochaev. The militiamen brutally grabbed Marfa and threw her down from the attic. Then they dragged her out of the house after intimidating the housewife. They dragged Marfa into the garden, raped her and pulled her out onto the road half dead and left her there. The following day Marfa was seen by residents and carried off to hospital; she was already unconscious and died shortly afterwards in hospital. . . . In similar fashion they killed in Pochaev, Lidia Tokmakova of Lipovaya Street . . . girls were raped, money taken away and people beaten until they lost consciousness. And so they roamed round the Lavra, all night through, like wild beasts, showing no respect even for old age: they robbed and raped Maria Andreevna Morozova, an aged nun, residing at Moscow K-203, Nizhnaya Pervomaiskaya, 24, apt. 4, Maria Gerasimchuk and Yustina Korolenko . . .

Any public gathering or demonstration with political overtones tends to incur similar brutality from police or internal security troops. On 14 April 1965, for example, a student demonstration for cultural freedom took place in central Moscow and, in the words of an anonymous participant,

At that moment, two plain-clothes security men jumped on the speaker from behind and pushed him down the steps where two more started twisting his arms behind his back. The students rushed to help him, but a lot more secret police had arrived. Many of the students were arrested at once. The leader of the demonstration managed to tear himself away but he was at once knocked to the ground by the security men, who began to drag him towards the car, hitting him at the same time.

'Anyone who loves art – help me!' he shouted, spitting out blood (his nose and lips had been split). At this the secret police and their sycophants burst out laughing. A group of students from the University were trying to rescue him, but without any success. He was fighting back with his feet and head, but already six people were dragging him. He was pushed into the car. We threw ourselves towards it, trying to open it, but we were pulled away. The car jumped forward in third gear and disappeared. Now we were fighting back. There was a scramble by the Writers' House. The trolley buses were at a standstill. The whole of Gertsen St was a battlefield. On one side were about 200 students, on the other about 100 people comprising secret police, security men, volunteer police, militia-men and Soviet writers. There were about 200 neutrals, who stood around shouting.

We managed to escape. Many others managed too, but not everybody . . .[19]

More recently, on 21 April 1968, a large group of Crimean Tatars, a people who have been demanding to return to their native Crimea whence Stalin expelled them, gathered in the Uzbek city of Chirchik to celebrate Lenin's birthday anniversary and in the words of a document signed by sixteen of their compatriots in Moscow on 23 April:[20]

About 1 p.m., when the fête was already in full swing – laughter and gay songs everywhere, music resounded, people gaily danced folk dances, noisy games were going on – the park was encircled by the military and police forces. The unthinkable began. Water-cannon brought along by the police started directing very sharp jets of some poisonous liquid onto the throng of people making merry. These jets knocked people off their feet. All persons hit by the jets got white stains on their clothes. . . . Policemen attacked people, many arms were dislocated by them and people were beaten, then shoved roughly into prison vans and driven away.

In the later evening the day's arbitrary actions were compounded by arrests of people in their homes, whereby even such persons were arrested who had not participated in the festivity. According to as yet incomplete information around 300 persons were arrested on 21 April. Many of them received physical injuries . . .

More recently still, the poet Natalya Gorbanevskaya (b. 1936) has provided an account of the violent break-up of a demonstration on Moscow's Red Square on 25 August 1968 against the

19. Full Russian text in *Possev*, 3 December 1965, English text in P. Reddaway's forthcoming anthology *Russia's Other Intellectuals*, Longmans, 1969. On the violent break-up of another Moscow demonstration, by V. Bukovsky and others on 22 January 1967, and on legal matters connected with it, see *Problems of Communism*, XVII, 4, 1968, pp. 31–6, and the important compilation by Pavel Litvinov (ed.), *Pravosudie ili rasprava?*, Overseas Publications Interchange Ltd, London, 1968.

20. Full Russian text in *Possev*, 6, 1968, pp. 10–11, English text in *Problems of Communism*, XVII, 4, 1968, pp. 92–3.

Soviet occupation of Czechoslovakia, staged by herself, Pavel Litvinov, Larisa Daniel and others.[21]

Other time-honoured police methods used against dissenters outside prisons and camps do not need physical violence. Persistent police spying is a common method of intimidation,[22] and the state's ultimate control of all jobs gives it a formidable weapon whose use has recently been documented by Sakharov and elsewhere.[23]

DISSENTERS AND MENTAL HOSPITALS

A mass of circumstantial evidence but as yet little first-hand testimony exists on this intricate subject, which the writer hopes to treat at length in due course. Documents 5 and 4 (Section 9), however, clearly indicate its nature, i.e. the imprisonment of certain sane dissenters without the inconvenience of a trial – what Document 1 calls 'the most shocking form of punishment' of all those used against dissenters. Moreover, a considerable amount of material is available by and about two such dissenters, Major-General Grigorenko (b. 1906)[24] and the poet-mathematician Alexander Esenin-Volpin (b. 1924).[25] But only one first-hand account of mental hospital conditions for political prisoners, written for Amnesty by Valerii Tarsis, as yet exists (although Tarsis's *Ward Seven** is only thinly fictionalized). While Tarsis's basic points are confirmed by circumstantial evidence, his account will not be published until it can be put beside other accounts. In any case, although the tendency conveniently to consider political

---

* Collins, 1965.

21. See *The Times*, 29 August 1968, and (Russian text) *Possev*, 9, 1968, p. 2.

22. See e.g. Chornovil's comic account in *Chornovil*, pp. 14–17.

23. See e.g. *Possev*, No. 6, 1968, pp. 2–5.

24. See *Possev*, 13 October 1967, No. 2, 1968, p. 8; No. 8, 1968, p. 2, and *Problems of Communism*, loc. cit., pp. 31–2, 44, 59–60, 72–3, all of which suggest that Grigorenko has never been insane, but was declared so because of his forthright opposition to injustice.

25. See his *A Leaf of Spring*, Thames & Hudson, 1961, *Novoe Russkoe Slovo*, New York, 13 October 1968, *Problems of Communism*, loc. cit., pp. 69–71, and *Possev*, No. 3, 1968, pp. 12–13, and No. 4, 1968, pp. 4–5, all of which suggest that while Esenin-Volpin may be highly-strung he is clearly not insane. Nevertheless he was forcibly put in a mental hospital by the authorities on 14 February 1968, at which time he was helping to organize protests against the Galanskov-Ginzburg trial.

or religious dissenters mad exists in all societies, it appears to have been especially strong in the history of Russia. Certainly it was sharply aggravated by some speeches of Khrushchev's in 1959. Having declared on one occasion 'We now have no prisoners in our jails for political reasons,' he added on another: 'A crime is a deviation from the generally recognized standards of behaviour, frequently caused by mental disorder. Can there be any diseases, mental disorders among certain men in communist society? Evidently there can be. If that is so, then there can be delinquencies characteristic of people of an abnormal mind.'[26] In other words social deviation is insanity.

These were the circumstances in which the instruction 'On the Immediate Hospitalization of Mentally Ill People Representing a Social Danger' reached the statute-book in 1961.[27] Article 1 of this instruction reads: 'If there is a clear danger to those around him or to himself from a mentally ill person the health organs have the right (by way of immediate psychiatric assistance) to place him in a psychiatric hospital without the consent of the person who is ill or his relatives or guardians.' This may be done, as Articles 5 and 6 make clear, by a single psychiatrist or ordinary doctor, and then the patient is detained or not, depending on the verdict of a panel of three psychiatrists. As no court verdict is required by this instruction it would appear to violate Articles 58–60 of the Russian Penal Code. This, however, as the Esenin-Volpin case shows, has not prevented its application, even after the issuing in February 1967 of an 'Instruction on the Procedure for Applying Compulsory Treatment and Other Medical Measures to Mentally Ill People who have Committed Socially Dangerous Acts'.[28] This new instruction provides for mental hospitals to admit such people only if a court order is among the documents

26. *Pravda*, 28 January 1959, p. 9, col. 3, and 24 May 1959, p. 2, col. 4. See on this subject Erich Goldhagen, 'The Glorious Future – Realities and Chimeras', in *Problems of Communism*, IX, 6, 1960, pp. 10–18.

27. See text in the compendium *Zakonodatel'stvo po zdravookhraneniyu* (*Legislation on Health Matters*), vol. 6, Moscow, 1963, and G. V. Morozov (ed.), *Praktika sudebno-psikhiatricheskoi ekspertizy* (*The Practice of Forenso-Psychiatric Investigation*), Research Handbook No. 6, Moscow, 1962.

28. Text in *Byulleten Verkhovnogo Suda SSSR*, No. 4, 1967. I am indebted to an unpublished article by A. Bilinsky for some of the material in this section.

presented. It thus seems possible that special police wings or rooms exist in certain mental hospitals, outside the jurisdiction of the Ministry of Health.

THE INSTITUTE OF FORENSIC PSYCHIATRY
NAMED AFTER SERBSKY

This Moscow institute, subordinate to the U.S.S.R. Ministry of Health, seems to continue to play a role in the struggle against Soviet dissenters, for several of the young intellectuals recently sentenced have been reported as spending a pre-trial period in it and it also features in Document 4 (Section 9). In July 1966 a member of Amnesty was received at it, after passing an armed guard, by the Director, Dr G. V. Morozov, who confirmed reports that the young writer Vladimir Bukovsky was currently detained there for psychiatric treatment although he had not undergone any trial. Bukovsky was subsequently released, but then later, in August 1967, sentenced to three years' imprisonment for organizing a demonstration (see note 19). As the court does not appear to have suggested that he had ever been either unbalanced or criminal in nature his stay in the Serbsky Institute remains unexplained.

The case of Galanskov, Ginzburg, Dobrovolsky and Lashkova may, however, provide a clue. For while all of them spent time in the institute before their trial in January 1968, Dobrovolsky gave evidence at it which was widely declared false and spoke very oddly, appearing to some witnesses to be under the influence of drugs.[29] In view of the recent testimony of the chief medical officer of the Czechoslovak judiciary during the Czech trials of the 1950s, Dr Rayman,[30] this supposition may be true. Rayman reported that strong-willed prisoners were put before an illuminated wall, confused by a barrage of questions, drugged with mescaline, and questioned until the desired answer was obtained.

---

29. See e.g. *Possev*, No. 2, 1968, p. 3. It could also be significant that Dr Morozov is the editor of the handbook mentioned in note 27 and also of *A Problem of Forensic Psychiatry: Organic Ailments of the Brain*, Moscow, 1965, and of *Current Problems in Psychiatry and Neuropathology*, Moscow, 1963.

30. *Rude Pravo*, Prague, 7 June 1968.

The responses were then fixed in the men's mind through another drug, so that they would be repeated at the trial.

Before leaving the subject of drugs, we may briefly note that a Ukrainian lawyer, L. H. Lukianenko (b. 1927), states in a closely argued document about the legality of advocating secession, written in Potma in May 1967, that drugs were used on him at his trial. He also refers to another case of their use in the Lvov prison.[31]

QUESTIONS OF LEGALITY

Questions of legality in the context of the treatment of Soviet dissenters tend, because of the deep inconsistencies of Soviet law in this field, to become highly technical and inconclusive. Nevertheless, strong denunciations of official practices, such as Lukianenko's, can be made on the basis of Soviet law, and a model of skill and wit in this genre is Chornovil's seventy-page petition to the legal authorities of the Ukraine.[32] Methodically his chapters cover the main ground: 'What is not punishable,' 'How are the "especially dangerous state criminals" discovered?', 'Search and arrests', 'Imprisonment, time limits for preliminary investigation', 'Violation of legal procedures in court', and so on. Sakharov takes Chornovil's argument a step further when, as noted earlier, he demands the abolition of all anti-constitutional laws. Examples of these are many of the laws on religion, and also Articles 190 (1) and 190 (3) of the Russian Penal Code, ratified in December 1966 despite the vigorous protest of Sakharov and other leading

31. Document to be printed in Michael Browne (ed.), *Ferment in the Ukraine*, Macmillan, 1969.

32. *Chornovil*, pp. 2–73. For similar materials on the Sinyavsky-Daniel trial see A. Ginzburg (ed.), *Belaya Kniga po Delu A. Sinyavskogo i Yu. Danielya*, Possev, Frankfurt, 1967, and L. Labedz and M. Hayward (eds.), *On Trial*, Collins, 1967, and, on the Galanskov-Ginzburg trial, *Problems of Communism*, XVII, 4, 1968, pp. 37–73. It may also be noted that Kandyba underlines in his earlier quoted appeal a tragic feature of Potma life by giving case-histories of various prisoners sentenced to 25 years who have already served over 15 (the normal maximum term for non-political prisoners), including a Czech citizen and lawyer of Ukrainian nationality, Dr Volodymyr Horbovyi, who was born in 1899. And another Ukrainian, Mykhaylo Horyn (mentioned above), describes in an important document (see Browne, op.cit.) the kangaroo court treatment to which he, Masyutko and Moroz were subjected in Potma on 16 July 1967, and which resulted for Horyn in a three-year prison sentence.

scientific and cultural figures. These additions have already been used to sentence Bukovsky and some of the pro-Czechoslovak protesters for their respective demonstrations mentioned above.

But apart from laws, instructions and regulations which infringe either the constitution (the supreme law) or, as in the case of forced committal to mental hospitals, the penal code or each other, there is also the phenomenon of secret and semi-secret legal acts. In this category stand two all-important documents: the camp ration scales and the 'Regulations on the Corrective-Labour Colonies and Prisons of the Ministry of Internal Affairs[33] of the R.S.F.S.R. (the Russian Republic)', drawn up, according to Karavansky (see above), by this ministry and its equivalents in the other constituent republics of the U.S.S.R., and ratified in 1961.[34] Both Marchenko and Larisa Daniel (see Documents 2 and 3) demand the publication of these documents as an essential step in the direction of prisoners being able to exercise whatever rights they may be granted in them. As, however, they both list some of the inhumanities which are actually *legalized* by the regulations, and as the ration-scales reported by Marchenko, Kandyba and others are clearly a form of prolonged torture – corresponding almost exactly to the average scales of Stalin's day – mere publication will not necessarily bring much improvement in the prisoners' lot.

But it would be a step forward. For at present a standard Soviet work like *Corrective-Labour Law*, edited by V. S. Tikunov (1966), can make no precise reference to these key documents or to their detailed provisions in critical areas, in its chapter on 'The régime in corrective-labour establishments' (pp. 165–87), or elsewhere. One author, however (pp. 48–51), cautiously approaches the problem by stressing the urgency of revising the outdated

33. Renamed Ministry for the Preservation of Public Order, or M.O.O.P., in 1962, and then again Ministry of Internal Affairs, or M.V.D., in 1968.

34. A rare reference to these regulations was made in *Vedomosti Verkhovnogo Soveta R.S.F.S.R.*, No. 37, 1961, p. 556, where a very brief and generalized summary of them appears. The summary does however mention that 'as a rule' prisoners should serve their terms in colonies or prisons near where they lived or were sentenced, a provision whose non-observance has especially angered Ukrainian prisoners in Potma, condemned for asking for the Ukraine's sovereign rights under the constitution to be granted in practice. Another reference to the regulations appears in ibid., 26, 1963, p. 592, where the introduction of a new form of colony is described.

corrective-labour codices of the 1930s, a process which appears to have made only slow progress since its initiation in 1959. Referring to 'the extra difficulties involved in the codification in view of the necessity of studying numerous sub-legal (mostly administrative) normative acts [*podzakonnykh* (*v osnovnom vedomstvennykh*) *normativnykh aktov*]', he continues:

after the codification there will be a considerable change in the relationship between laws and sub-legal acts in the field of corrective-labour legislation. The law will occupy the leading position among the sources of corrective-labour legislation. But even then it will remain to regulate a certain part of the provisions in the field of punishment imposed on the basis of sub-legal normative acts.

This is an indication of some of the main legal aspects of the Soviet treatment of dissenters. Further discussion of them would, however, take us well beyond the bounds of this essay.

THE INCIPIENT SOVIET CIVIL RIGHTS MOVEMENT

Certain common threads and interconnexions will have become apparent even in such a brief survey as this: they seem to imply an incipient civil rights movement. For there is a platform common to the Moscow-Leningrad radicals, the Ukrainian intellectuals and the religious groups: their unanimous demand (no longer a frightened request)[35] for the observance, and better definition, of legality. Here the Constitution, with all its faults, serves as a base. Furthermore, there are the increasing links between the three groups, a growing sense that their fate is indivisible. To mention a few examples, in Potma the Ukrainians mix with Daniel, Sinyavsky and various Leningraders. In Moscow, Galanskov's literary-political journal *Phoenix 1966* publishes the long account of the resistance of the Pochaev monks to persecution quoted above. In the same city, the Orthodox Krasnov-Levitin (b. 1915 – see Document 1), who has shown since 1959, in his 'underground'

---

35. In addition to writing Document 2, Marchenko, for example, has taken the offensive against the neo-stalinist editor of the *Literary Gazette*, A. Chakovsky, in an open letter. See *Possev*, No. 6, 1968, p. 7. In August 1968, however, he was reimprisoned for support of the Czechoslovak democratization – see documents in *Problems of Communism*, No. 5, 1968, pp. 59–62.

writings,[36] his understanding of the indivisibility of freedom, champions the civil rights of Baptists, Orthodox, atheists, writers, Crimean Tatars and, at his trial, Galanskov. In the Ukraine 139 Ukrainian intellectuals and workers sign a protest letter to the Soviet leaders about the illegalities not only of the Ukrainian trials but also of the Galanskov-Ginsburg trial.[37] In the foothills of the Urals, at Kirov, one of the most persistent unofficial Orthodox writers, Boris Talantov (b. c. 1910), denounces the same trial and continues: 'I therefore deem it my duty to lodge a determined protest against the arbitrary way in which nowadays court trials are held in camera, against the persecution of people for their beliefs, and against the inhuman confinement of political prisoners in prisons and camps.'[38] And everywhere, as information spreads more rapidly – to the dismay of the police – the U.N. Declaration of Human Rights is quoted and re-quoted.[39]

Nevertheless the re-stalinizing police remain strong and the obstacles to progress many: none of the protests have yet been carried by the censored Soviet news media; no one yet has enough information to make even a rough estimate of the total number of Soviet political and religious prisoners (although the relevant units would seem likely to be tens of thousands, this would not include the possibly enormous numbers of people exiled to remote areas,

36. See in particular two collections of his articles, both edited by Arkhiepiskop Ioann San-Frantisskii, published by Ikhthus in Paris and printed by Possev Verlag in Frankfurt, *Zashchita very v SSSR*, 1966, and *Dialog s tserkovnoi Rossiei*, 1967; also translations of two of his documents in *Problems of Communism*, XVII, 4, 1968, pp. 104–9, and of others in Bourdeaux, *Patriarchs and Prophets*.

37. Text in *Possev*, No. 12, 1968, p. 58, and in English in M. Browne, op.cit.

38. See the abridged document in *Problems of Communism*, loc. cit., pp. 111–12, and full text in M. Bourdeaux, *Patriarch and Prophets*. Another Orthodox, Father Sergi Zheludkov, has shown similar solidarity with the Moscow radicals. See his letters in *Possev*, No. 11, 1968, pp. 10–11 and No. 12, 1968, p. 57, and in *Novoe Russkoe Slovo*, New York, 2 December 1968.

39. After this paper was finished three issues of a 'Chronicle of Current Events' entitled 'Human Rights Year in the Soviet Union', and collating very detailed material on recent trials etc. which have violated the Declaration, reached the West. Number 1, dated 30 April 1968 and some 5,000 words in length, has been published in extracts in *Possev*, No. 12, 1968, pp. 11–14, and contains the information given in footnote (7); No. 2, dated 30 June and even longer than No. 1, has appeared in *Novoe Russkoe Slovo*, 24 November 1968; and number 3, dated 31 August, has appeared in *Novoe Russkoe Slovo*, 3 November 1968. All three are very remarkable compilations which reveal the determination of the civil rights movement to resist restalinization.

some 'for ever' [*navechno*],[40] or living as exiles without civil rights in the areas of the dismantled camps where they were previously imprisoned [*rezhim vol'nogo poseleniya*]); and only the religious dissent involves the workers and peasants on a significant scale. Even so, a broad civil rights movement may well at this stage make more progress than the various underground political parties which have appeared of late in, especially, the Ukraine and Leningrad, and which can be eliminated by the police without too much difficulty. The fact that a great abundance of material was available to write this paper in itself denotes a great change. It will in fact become steadily less easy for Soviet spokesmen to denounce the beam in, say, the Greek eye without looking first at their own Potma and Vladimir motes – about which they must expect increasing concern from international bodies in the field of human rights. Amnesty International, for example, has a fast-growing number of Soviet names to enter on the newly instituted international register of alleged torturers in different parts of the world, and it has also tried to gain access for its observers at important Soviet trials. Such observers may in due course be admitted, since Litvinov and Larisa Daniel, for instance, in their well-known appeal to world and Soviet opinion during the Galanskov-Ginzburg trial, included the words 'Demand a new trial in conformity with all legal norms and in the presence of international observers!'[41] And a role to be played – indeed already being played – by non-Soviet news media in helping the Soviet civil rights movement to outwit one of its chief bugbears and targets, censorship, and reach the Soviet public, is indicated in the final paragraph of the same appeal: 'We address this appeal to the Western progressive press and ask that it be published and broadcast by radio as soon as possible. We are not sending this request to Soviet newspapers because that is hopeless.'

In conclusion it may not be out of place to quote a passage from Anatolii Marchenko:

I should like my testimony on Soviet camps and prisons for political prisoners to become known to humanists and progressive people of

40. The great writer Alexander Solzhenitsyn describes getting this treatment after the death of Stalin. See *Grani*, Frankfurt, No. 69, 1968, p. 1.
41. *Problems of Communism*, loc. cit., p. 44.

other countries – those who raise their voice in defence of political prisoners in Greece and Portugal, in the South African Republic and in Spain. Let them ask their Soviet colleagues in the struggle against anti-humanism: 'What have you done in order that your political prisoners, in your own country, are at least not "educated" by hunger?'

Documents

DOCUMENT I
A GENERAL PROTEST AGAINST REPRESSION

Letter to the Presidium of the Consultative Meeting of the Communist Parties in Budapest.

In the last few years several political trials have taken place in our country. Their essential significance consists in the fact that people were tried for their beliefs in violation of their basic civil rights. That is precisely why these trials have seen such serious abuses of legal rights, the most important abuse being the absence of open trials.

Public opinion does not wish to tolerate such lawlessness any longer; it has caused indignation and protest which mounted from trial to trial. A great number of individual and collective letters were sent to the judicial, government and party institutions, including the central committee of the C.P.S.U. These letters have remained unanswered. However, those who were most active in their protests received a reply in the form of notices terminating their employment, summonses to the K.G.B. with the threat of arrest, and, finally, the most shocking form of punishment, compulsory confinement in a mental asylum. These illegal and inhuman acts cannot have any positive result. On the contrary, they increase tension and give rise to further indignation. We consider it our duty to draw attention to the fact that there are in the prisons and camps several thousands of political prisoners about whom almost no one knows. They find themselves in inhuman conditions of compulsory labour on a semi-starvation diet, abandoned to the arbitrary power of the administration. After the termination of their sentences they are subject to extra-legal, and often illegal, persecution: restrictions as to where they can live, and administrative supervision, measures which put a free man in the position of an exile.

We would also like to draw your attention to the discrimination against national minorities and to the political persecution of people struggling for equal national rights, which has manifested itself especially clearly in the case of the Crimean Tatars.

You may know that many communists in foreign countries and in our own country have often expressed their critical views about the political persecutions of recent years. We ask the participants of the consultative meeting to assess fully the danger which results from the complete disregard of human rights in our country.

24 February 1968.

DR PAVEL LITVINOV (a physicist and grandson of Maxim Litvinov), Moscow, K-1, ul. Alekseya Tolstogo 8, kv. 78;

LARISA DANIEL (a philologist and wife of the writer Yuli Daniel), Moscow, V-261, Leninsky prospekt 85, kv. 3;

ALEXEI KOSTERIN (a writer and Party member since 1916), Moscow, M. Gruzinskaya 31, kv. 70;

DR ZAMIRA ASANOVA (a doctor and leader of the Crimean Tatars), Yangi-Kurgan, Fergana region;

VICTOR KRASIN (an economist), Moscow, Belomorskaya ul. 24, kv. 25;

ILYA GABAI (a teacher), Moscow, A-55, Novo-Lesnaya ul. 18, kor. 2, kv. 8;

PYOTR YAKIR (a historian), Moscow, Zh-280, Avtozavodskaya 5, kv. 75;

BORIS SHRAGIN (a philosopher), Moscow, G-117, Pogodinka 2/3, kv. 91;

ANATOLI LEVITIN-KRASNOV (a religious publicist), Moscow, Zh-377, 3-ya Novokuzminskaya ul. 23;

YULI KIM (a teacher), Zh-377, Ryazansky prospekt 73, kv. 90;

YURI GLAZOV (a linguist), Moscow, V-421, Leninsky prospekt 101/164, kv. 4;

Pyotr Grigorenko (a construction engineer and former Major-General), Moscow, G-21, Komsomolsky prospekt 14/1, kv. 46.

(Russian text in *Possev*, No. 3, 1968, p. 7)

DOCUMENT 2
OPEN LETTER BY A. MARCHENKO

To:

The Chairman of the Red Cross Society of the U.S.S.R., G. A. Mitiryov;

the Minister of Health of the U.S.S.R., B. V. Petrovsky;

the Director of the Food Institute at the Academy of Medical Sciences, A. A. Pokrovsky;

the Patriarch of All Russia, Aleksi;

the President of the Academy of Sciences of the U.S.S.R., M. V. Keldysh;

the President of the Academy of Medical Sciences of the U.S.S.R., V. D. Timakov;

the Director of the Institute of State and Law, Chkhikvadze;

the Rector of Moscow State University, I. G. Petrovsky;

the Chairman of the Board of the U.S.S.R. Journalists' Union Zimyanin;

the First Secretary of the Board of the U.S.S.R. Writers' Union, K. Fedin;

the writers K. Simonov, R. Gamzatov, R. Rozhdestvensky, Ye. Yevtushenko.

(Copies to the U.N. Human Rights Commission and to the International Human Rights Conference of the U.N.O.)

Five months ago I completed a book, *My Testimony* (*Moi pokazaniya*),[42] about the six years (1960–66) which I spent in Vladimir prison and in camps for political prisoners. In the introduction I write that:

42. Extracts were published in French in the journal *L'Express*, Paris, 30 September – 6 October 1968, and full publication is planned in Russian and other languages.

contemporary Soviet camps for political prisoners are as horrible as were Stalin's. In some respects they are better, in some respects worse.

Everybody should know about this.

Both those who want to know the truth but instead get false, glossy newspaper articles lulling the reader's conscience.

And those who don't want to know and who shut their eyes and stop their ears, in order to be able to justify themselves later and to show their clean record: 'Good Lord, and we never knew. . . .' If they have even a scrap of social conscience and genuine love for their country they will take a stand in its defence, as Russia's true sons have always done.

I should like my testimony on Soviet camps and prisons for political prisoners to become known to humanists and progressive people of other countries – those who raise their voice in defence of political prisoners in Greece and Portugal, in the South African Republic and in Spain. Let them ask their Soviet colleagues in the struggle against anti-humanism: 'What have you done in order that your political prisoners in your own country are at least not 'educated' by hunger?

I have done my best to make my book known to the public. However, there has been no reaction at all so far (except for a conversation about my 'anti-social activities' to which I was invited by a K.G.B. officer). Conditions in the camps remain the same. Thus I have been forced to turn to certain personalities who through their social position are among those most responsible for the state of our society and its level of humanity and legality.

You should know the following:

In the camps and prisons of our country there are thousands of political prisoners. Most of them were sentenced behind closed doors; there have been virtually no really open trials (apart from those of war-criminals); in all cases a fundamental principle of legal procedure – publicity – has been violated. Thus society controlled, and controls, neither the observance of legality nor the extent of political repression.

The situation of the political prisoners is generally the same as that of the criminal convicts, and in some respects it is considerably worse: political prisoners are at best held in 'strict' régime conditions, while for the criminals there is an 'ordinary' régime and an even lighter one; criminals may be released after serving two-thirds or half of their time, while the political prisoners have to serve every single day of their sentence.

Thus the political prisoners are treated in all respects like the most dangerous criminals and recidivists. There is no juridical and legal distinction.

The political prisoners are as a rule people who before being arrested were engaged in socially useful labour: engineers, workers, literary men, artists, scientists. In the camp, by way of 're-educational measures', they have to do forced labour, whereby the camp administration uses work as a means of punishment: weakly persons are forced to perform heavy physical labour; intellectuals are compelled to do unskilled physical work. Failure to fulfil the norm is regarded as a violation of the régime and serves as a pretext for various administrative punishments – veto on visitors, punishment cell, solitary confinement.

The most powerful means of influencing the prisoners is hunger. The usual rations are such as to make a person feel perpetual want of food, perpetual malnutrition. The daily camp ration contains 2,400 calories (enough for a seven- to eleven-year-old child), and has to suffice for an adult doing physical work, day after day for many years, sometimes as many as fifteen or twenty-five years! Those calories are supplied mainly by black bread (700 gm. a day). The convicts never even set eyes on fresh vegetables, butter, and many other indispensable products; these products are even prohibited from sale at the camp stall (as also sugar).

Let me state right away: the camp food as well as the camp clothes are paid for by the prisoners themselves from the earnings accredited to them. (Fifty per cent is deducted at once for the upkeep of the camp: barracks, equipment, fences, watch-towers, etc.) Only five roubles* a month – out of the money that remains after all deductions – can be spent on goods (including tobacco) at the stall. But one may be deprived even of this right, to spend seventeen copecks a day, 'for violation of the régime'. For example, the imprisoned historian Rendel (ten years for participation in an illegal Marxist circle) was banned from the stall for two months for bringing supper to sick comrades in the barracks; so was the imprisoned writer Sinyavsky, for exchanging a few

* Slightly over £2 at the official exchange rate.

words with his friend Daniel when the latter was in the camp prison.

To punish a prisoner for 'violating the camp régime', e.g., for failure to fulfil the work quota, he may be put on the 'severe' food ration – 1,300 calories[43] (enough for an infant of one to three years). This was the case, for example, with the writer Daniel and the engineer Ronkin (seven years for illegal Marxist activity) at the end of the summer of 1967.

Food parcels from relatives are 'not authorized' for prisoners sentenced to the 'strict' régime; only by way of encouragement for good behaviour (that is, repentance, denunciation, collaboration with the administration) do the camp authorities sometimes allow a prisoner to receive a food parcel – but not before he has served half his sentence, not more than four times a year, and not over five kilograms!

Thus the camp administration wields a powerful means of exerting physical pressure on the political prisoners – a whole system of escalation of hunger. The application of this system results in emaciation and avitaminosis.

Some prisoners are driven by permanent malnutrition to kill and eat crows, and, if they are lucky, dogs. In the autumn of 1967 one prisoner of the 2nd camp division at Dubrovlag found a way of getting potatoes while he was in the hospital section; he overate and died. (The potatoes were raw).

Hunger reigns even more harshly in Vladimir prison and in the 'special régime camps', where there are also numerous political prisoners.

In comparison with the permanent malnutrition, other 'means of influence' look relatively harmless. One must however mention

43. In another document (see note 35) Marchenko breaks down the normal ration as six cupfuls of thin gruel, two cupfuls of soup made with rotten cabbage, and a piece of boiled cod the size of a match-box, all this containing only 20 gm. of fat, plus 700 gm. of black bread and 15 gm. of sugar. The 'severe' ration contains 400 gm. of cabbage soup, two cupfuls of thin gruel, the same size piece of cod and 450 gm. of black bread. We may note here that the Japanese concentration camp at Tha Makham on the River Kwai in Thailand had in 1942–3 a daily ration norm of 700 gm. of rice, 600 of vegetables, 100 of meat, 20 of sugar, 20 of salt and 15 of oil (with similarly few chances of buying extra food), this amounting to about 3,400 calories. Even here, though, vitamin deficiency diseases were very common. See article by Ian Watt in the *Observer*, 1 September 1968.

a few of them: prohibiting meetings with one's relatives; complete shaving of the head; prohibiting the wearing of one's own clothes (including warm underwear in winter); obstructing creative work and the performance of religious rites.

Prisoners' letters of complaint and petitions, addressed to the Procuracy, the Presidium of the Supreme Soviet of the U.S.S.R., or the Central Committee of the C.P.S.U. are returned without fail to the camp administration: the highest organs send them to the Ministry for the Preservation of Public Order [M.O.O.P.] or to the Main Administration of Places of Confinement [G.U.M.Z.], and from there after a multi-stage journey round the departments they somehow or other always end up in the hands of those against whom the complaints were directed, 'so that they can be checked'. All complaints naturally end in the same way with the camp administration's answer that 'the assertions have not been confirmed', and that 'the punishment was justified', and the position of the petitioner becomes unbearable. Sometimes he is even transferred to the [camp] prison or to solitary confinement for his latest 'violation of the régime'. Therefore the 'educators-cum-officers' often maliciously say to the dissatisfied prisoner: 'Go on, lodge a complaint against us; go on, write, it's your right.' Others, more simple-minded, warn him: 'Well, why protest? You know yourself the administration can always find a reason to punish any prisoner. You'll only harm yourself; better put up with it . . .'

And indeed, 'The Regulations for Camps and Prisons', passed by the Supreme Soviet in 1961, give the camp administration practically unlimited opportunities to apply physical and moral pressure. Prohibition of food parcels, a ban on purchases from the camp stall, starvation rations, banning of visits, punishment cell, handcuffs, solitary confinement – all this is legalized by the 'Regulations' and applied to political prisoners. The camp administration finds these measures much to its taste, all the more so as among the 'educators' are not a few officials of the stalinist concentration camps, used to unlimited arbitrary power (which, incidentally, was quite in line with their instructions at that time).

As the prisoners lack all rights they are driven to dreadful and disastrous forms of protest: hunger strikes, self-mutilation, suicide

– in broad daylight the prisoner goes out of bounds towards the barbed wire, and there the guard shoots him 'for attempted flight'.

Some among you bear direct responsibility for the existing situation; the responsibility of others is determined by their public position. But I turn to you as my fellow citizens: we are all equally responsible to our motherland, to the young generation, to the country's future. It suffices that the generation of the thirties and forties put up with crimes committed 'in the name of the people'; it is impossible and impermissible to display again the criminal indifference which then turned the whole nation into accomplices in bloody crimes.

I appeal to you to:

Demand a public investigation into the situation of political prisoners.

Demand the wide publication of the 'Regulations on Camps and Prisons'; try to have special rules made for political prisoners.

Demand the publication of the food rations for prisoners.

Demand immediate dismissal from 'educational' work of the former staff of stalinist concentration camps and of such camp officials as have more recently displayed cruelty and inhumanity towards prisoners. Demand a public trial for them.

It is our civic duty, the duty of our human conscience, to put a stop to crimes against humanity. For crime begins not with the smoking chimneys of crematoria, nor with the steamers packed with prisoners bound for Magadan. Crime begins with civic indifference.

2nd April 1968
Aleksandrov (Vladimir Region)
Novinskaya Street, 27.   A. MARCHENKO

(Russian text in *Possev*, No. 6, 1968, pp. 5–7.)

DOCUMENT 3

AN OPEN LETTER FROM LARISA DANIEL ABOUT THE ILL-TREATMENT OF HER HUSBAND IN POTMA

To:

Leaders of the Party and Government;
members of the Judicial Organs;
the Collegium of Moscow Advocates;
the Academy of Medical Science of the U.S.S.R.;
the Soviet Red Cross;
the Secretariat of the Union of Soviet Writers;
the Moscow section of the Union of Soviet Writers;
the Leningrad section of the Union of Soviet Writers;
the Presidium of the Academy of Sciences of the U.S.S.R.;
the Editors of newspapers;
the members of the Supreme Soviet of the U.S.S.R.;
the members of the Supreme Soviet of the Russian Federal
    Republic.

I appeal to the Government, to the representatives of (professional) associations, to lawyers and doctors, to scholars and writers, to put a stop to the inhuman and illegal actions of those in charge of the corrective-labour camp P.O. Box 385–17, which is under the command of Comrade Annienkov, and in which my husband, the writer Yuli Daniel, is detained. I beg them to put a stop to the arbitrary acts which endanger the health and life of my husband and of other detainees, and which discredit our Government and our legal system.

Daniel is at present detained in the prison of the camp, where he is to stay for six months. These are the facts which have led to his being treated so severely: the warders forbade Daniel to use an anti-mosquito ointment and ordered him to give up his supply of it. This is nothing new: already in the thirties, during the period of the notorious 'Violations of Socialist Legality', those in charge of labour camps were empowered to torment the prisoners in this manner.

Daniel refused to obey the order. Thereupon three warders fell upon him and started twisting his arms. Daniel naturally resisted. They overpowered him, threw him onto the ground, battered his face, handcuffed him up in the prison hut of the camp in which the detainees are subject to so-called rigorous discipline.

This means that they may not lie on their bunks from reveille to lights-out, that the hut is cold and damp, even in summer, and that their food is limited to a punitive ration. Daniel is in poor health: he has a chronic inflammation of the ear, aggravated during his imprisonment, for he has had no medical care, has not been allowed to see an ear specialist or – in spite of repeated requests – to use the necessary medicines. He also suffers from after-effects of his serious war wound and from the exhaustion induced by under-nourishment in camp. This alarms me, and makes me apprehensive for my husband's health and for his life.

Not that the punishment inflicted on Daniel is in any way exceptional in a camp where political prisoners are kept. Any arbitrary decision by the Camp Commandment has the force of law: he can reduce the rations, cut the number of visits from relations or stop them altogether, forbid parcels, letters, tobacco, books and, in the last resort, order the punishment cell, the handcuffs, the 'rigorous discipline'. Since the Camp Commandant is subject to no control and the prisoners have no rights, living as they do cut off from society and the outside world, the Commandant can always justify his decisions by the alleged 'bad behaviour' of the prisoner, or accuse him of failing to reach his production quota. In these circumstances, the prisoner's life and health depend entirely upon whether the Commandant, the instructors, the warders happen to be good or bad, for his human rights are in no way ensured or safeguarded.

In 1967, the fiftieth anniversary of the Soviet régime, prisoners are subjected to what the Soviet corrective labour code of the twenties defined as torture.

All this, as I see it, should provoke serious thought and lead to insistence on socialist legality being upheld in places of detention. The only way to ensure the rule of law and of humanity is to publish the regulations which apply to such places of detention, and clearly define the amount of the rations. These regulations ought to be known not only in the camps but also outside, and prisoners should have the right to report violations of the rules, and arbitrary acts, and this not only to the Camp Commandant.

In my particular case, I request a public inquiry into what has taken place, and the immediate release of my husband from his illegal confinement in the camp prison. There should also be a public inquiry into the confinement in the same prison of the university student L. Rendel, punished merely because he asked to see the camp authorities in order to protest against the manner in which it is administered.

Over a month ago, I sent a letter to a number of writers: to the members of the Presidium and Secretariat of the Union of Soviet Writers, Fedin, Surkov, Tvardovsky, Sobolev, Chakovsky, Leonov, Tikhonov. In that letter I described the conditions in the camp in which Daniel is detained, and the abuses which are committed in it. Had these writers felt disturbed by this information and acted upon it, it is likely that Daniel would not have suffered the punishment inflicted upon him at the beginning of June. As things are, I have good reason to believe that this punishment inflicted upon my husband is directly related to the letter I addressed to the writers, a letter which provoked no reaction on their part and to which I have received no reply. It is because of the inertia of public opinion that irresponsible people in positions of authority are able to commit abuses and bring violence into our lives.

(17 June 1967)

(A long account of her journey to Potma by Larisa Daniel was published in German in *Die Zeit*, Hamburg, 22 September 1967, and in English in *Atlas*, New York, December 1967, pp. 22–6. Permission to make the journey was obtained only after many attempts, and at the meeting with her husband, strictly limited to one hour, she was not allowed to give him even a few oranges. This account is probably the letter referred to above.)

DOCUMENT 4

BAPTIST APPEAL TO WORLD OPINION FOR DEFENCE AGAINST PERSECUTION (Extract)

To:

The General-Secretary of the U.N.O., Mr U Thant;

the Committee on Human Rights;

the International Committee for the Protection of Children.

Copies to:

The General-Secretary of the C.C. C.P.S.U., Comrade L. I. Brezhnev;

the President of the Presidium of the Supreme Soviet of the U.S.S.R., Comrade N. V. Podgorny;

the Council of the Baptist World Alliance.

From the Council of Relatives of Prisoners, members of the Church of Evangelical Christians-Baptists (E.C.B.), convicted for the Word of God in the U.S.S.R.

Dear Mr U Thant:

By reason of the unceasing persecution of believers of the Evangelical-Baptist faith in the U.S.S.R. and the lack of an answer to a letter sent previously by the Council of Relatives of Prisoners of the E.C.B. in the U.S.S.R., we are compelled to turn again to you. All of our efforts before the Government of our country to the present day remain without result. It evades a direct answer to the pleas of the relatives of prisoners. Because of this, we have decided to appeal to you, as to the world's highest instance.

Believers of the Evangelical-Baptist faith (E.C.B.) in the U.S.S.R. have for many years experienced all possible sorts of repression. Therefore we – mothers, wives, children and relatives of prisoners who are members of the Church of the E.C.B. convicted for the Word of God – turn to you, inasmuch as you, by the power of the statutes of the U.N. are called to defend the elementary rights of man regardless of nationality, race or religion.

[The numbered sections I to 4 of the letter are here omitted for reasons of space.]

5. MANIFESTATION OF TORTURE OF BELIEVERS

Urgent communique to the Government from the Kiev congregation of Baptists

With deep sorrow we advise you that on Thursday, 30 March 1967, in the house of our fellow believer Nikolai Pavlovich Shelestun, 36 Ostrovskoye St., Novaia Boiarka, Kiev Oblast, where we were gathered for a worship meeting (it was his turn), at 20.30 hrs., a district lieutenant of the police, in uniform, arrived with seven men in civilian clothes, disrupting the meeting. One of them was the chief of the Boiarsk G.O.M. [ordinary police], two men introduced themselves as from the U.O.O.P. [Directorate for the Preservation of Public Order] of Kiev, and the remainder we do not know.

Trying to note down all those present, they seized the passport of the owner of the house and said, 'You will pay for this,' and ordered him to appear at the Boiarsk police-station.

On 2 April 1967 at 16.45 hrs he appeared at the Boiarsk police-station. At 17.00 hrs he was summoned to the office of the chief of police, with whom were the procurator and district officials. When N. P. Shelestun, the father of two children, had been seated on a chair not far from the table and was asking him his name, the chief of police, coming up behind him, said, 'You have tormented us, now we will torment you,' and struck him on the head with his fist. Sitting by the table, the procurator also began to strike him on the head, face, back of the neck, and ears from the other side. To the question, why are you doing this to me, they, using uncensored words, answered, 'We'll beat the guts out of you and we won't be called to account.' Then the chief of police fell to his knees in front of the bruised [prisoner], folded his hands, and sneered, 'Now ask God to save you from us.' N. P. Shelestun fell from the chair to the floor from the blows, losing consciousness. After the first beatings they sat him on the chair by the hair, brought an official report with a blank space and ordered him to sign. For his refusal to sign they again began to beat him, saying, 'Sign!' In the official report which they gave him to sign there was written, 'At the religious meeting in the house of N. P.

Shelestun anti-Soviet leaflets were read.' For refusal to sign this falsehood they again subjected him to beating. When he had fallen on the floor unconscious, the policemen continued to kick him. As blood was flowing from him, the chief of police said to him, 'Wipe off the blood!' The chief of police took away two handkerchiefs soaked with the blood which was flowing from his mouth and nose. At 19.00 hrs, threatening to deliver the beaten man to Kiev, Korolenko 15 (the police-station), when they had searched his pockets and seized his personal things, they sent him home, saying, 'Warn your friends that the same fate awaits them.'

Inasmuch as we have seen N. P. Shelestun beaten and ill and have questioned a witness, and have heard and seen the exercise of arbitrary justice by officials, and also have in hand a report of an eyewitness of his beating issued in the dispensary of the Kiev Oblast Bureau of Judicial Medical Investigation on 3 April 1967, No. 2247, we communicate to you that these actions constitute continuing physical struggle and violence against religious convictions.

By commission of the Kiev church of the E.C.B., consisting of 400 people.

5 April 1967.   Signatures: 78 people.

*Concerning torture applied to the invalids
A. I. Kovalchuk of Rovno (1963),
and A. Ya. Pavlenko of Odessa (1966).*

During the examination of A. I. Kovalchuk in 1963 torture was applied. They ruptured his spleen and blood and bile flowed. He was released by reason of the hopeless state of his health and was rehabilitated. In the process of treatment he was given three and a half litres of blood and ninety litres of glucose and intravenous liquid. In June 1966 he was again arrested with the collusion of the investigator who had tortured him, who said, 'We are going to take out of you the blood which they gave you.' He was able to escape from his hands, but to this day is deprived of the right to life: to this day they have not returned his passport to him, nor his pension booklet, and in order to remain alive he has had to hide.

A. Ya. Pavlenko was arrested on 11 June 1966, while sick, and on 11 August he was taken to court. After the torture which was applied during the investigation, he was reduced to a point where he was unrecognizable. While in prison with a high temperature (102·2° F), Pavlenko repeatedly asked that medical aid be given him. But instead he was beaten during the investigation until he lost consciousness. After one of a series of interrogations he regained consciousness on the operating table in the hospital. He told of this for everyone to hear in court. (Statement of believers of Odessa for the attention of A. Ya. Gorkin, President of the Supreme Court of the U.S.S.R.)

N. K. Khmara of Barnaul (1964), O. P. Vibe of Karaganda (1964), Vins of Aktiubinsk, Taran of Ussuriisk, Rizhenko of Cherkessk, Kucherenko of Nikolaev (during interrogation), and others have died of tortures and the unbearable conditions which are created in prisons, camps and exile.

Even during the court trial itself there is torture of our imprisoned relatives. For example: the trial of the President of the Council of Churches, G. K. Kriuchkov, and the Secretary of the Council of Churches of the E.C.B., G. P. Vins, which took place in Moscow on 29–30 November 1966. Almost none of the believers were admitted into the courtroom. The audience was carefully selected and of a hostile disposition. There were cries in the courtroom, and noise. In such conditions the first day of the trial lasted from 10 a.m. to 9 p.m. G. K. Kriuchkov and G. P. Vins were exhausted, inasmuch as during the course of the entire day they were not even allowed a drink. On the second day the trial began at 10 a.m. and concluded at 2 a.m. All requests for adjournment of the trial to the following day were denied. Therefore, with regard to their physical exhaustion and the conditions created in the court, they were, in fact, deprived of the possibility of making the defence they had decided to make themselves.

The court was unable to establish a single proven crime by them, but they were sentenced to three years' deprivation of freedom.

6. MAINTENANCE CONDITIONS OF PRISONERS OF THE E.C.B. IN CAMPS AND PRISONS

Especially difficult conditions are created for believers of the E.C.B. in the camps.

1. Contrary to the rules of the régime of corrective camps, they are deprived of the right to correspond with friends and relatives. Letters in which the word 'God' or other phrases of religious content appear are held back and not permitted. We have the statement of the prisoner Nikolai Velichko of Kiev; the statements of the prisoners Abram Abramovich Gizbrekht, Vasilii Niko-laevich Rudenko, Ivan Maksimovich Enns, Peter Petrovich Leven, Peter Yakovlevich Yants, who completed their terms for faith in God in Barnaul, Altai Region, P. O. Box UB-14/1, division 7, brigade 32; the letter of S. T. Golev and N. F. Popov, who completed their terms in the camp P. O. Box 25/6. In the Kaluga camp the authorities burned a packet of letters before the eyes of Mikhail Khorev, and did not allow him to read them. We have the statement of the mother of the twenty-year-old prisoner Vera Petrovna Shuportiak that she receives no letters from her daughter, etc.

2. The general policy that imprisoned believers of the E.C.B. are not allowed Bibles and Gospels, as dangerous books, in the camps. The whole world accepts the fact that that the Holy Books are the first necessity of every believer, and to all appearances their prohibition does not feature in the rules of the régime of the camps. This is nothing else but a special order of the C.C. C.P.S.U. to the organs of the Committee of State Security [K.G.B.]. The Secretary of the Council of Churches of the E.C.B., Georgii Petrovich Vins, was deprived of his Bible upon entry into the camp. This has happened to all of the prisoners of the E.C.B. in the U.S.S.R.

3. Prisoners of the E.C.B. are deprived of the right to fulfil their spiritual necessities – evening devotions. Other democratic countries even provide chaplains out of state funds for prisoners in camps, but we are deprived of the right to have even our own ministers to fulfil these needs. Where is the legal basis of this?

4. Prisoners of the E.C.B. are deprived of the right to pray in prisons and camps. We have statements to this effect from prisoners of the E.C.B. In a camp in Dnepropetrovsk Oblast, village of Appolonovka, Soloniansk district, the E.C.B. believer Pavel Overchuk was put in the detention cell on 26 April this year. On that day the commanding officer told his mother, who had arrived for a visit, that her son had been placed in a detention cell and had been deprived of the right to visits and correspondence for six months because morning and evening he prayed and talked about Christ. Previously Overchuk had not received mail for three months. Thus the mother, who had spent her means, returned with nothing, and Pavel Overchuk was not allowed to receive food packages for nine months. The mother also stated that her son refused to promise to stop praying and talking about Christ, and if he did not change his convictions after detention cell he would be given a re-trial and his sentence extended to eight years.

The *shizo* (punishment isolator) threatens many prisoners for the same reason. Many have been and are in it; they even threaten the old seventy-one-year-old prisoner Sergei Terentevich of Riazan with it.

We have data on this from many camps and prisons.

5. Deprivation of the right to periodic mail and visits on grounds of refusal to work on Sunday.

Vera Petrovna Shuportiak, who is in a camp at Potma Station, was deprived of visits and two months' periodic mail for refusal to work on Sunday, although prior to this she was working up to twelve hours a day. She is very weak, starved.

The same has been the case with the prisoners Gizbrekht, Enns, Leven, Yants and Rudenko in the camp mentioned above, and others.

6. E.C.B. believers in the camps are terrorized by constant interrogations and threats, and are forbidden to see each other.

7. Conditions detrimental to health are established for imprisoned believers of the E.C.B.

Viktor Alekseevich Bratushko, born 1929, was convicted under Article 142, Paragraph 2 of the Russian Code, and is in the Dnepropetrovsk Oblast. From the time of his imprisonment on 21 May 1966 he became ill with stomach and heart trouble, and a head cold. The condition of his health is poor. He was not in condition to make use of a two-hour visit because of severe headache.

Aleksei Kozorezov (prisoner), mentioned above, languishing in a cell without daylight, has contracted heart trouble. Boris Yevtikhievich Filippov, who is ill, is languishing in a camp, as is Lidiia Govorun, who is seriously ill and is in Potma, arrested and condemned as a member of the Council of Relatives of Prisoners for a request concerning the liberation of prisoners, her son Seriozha having been spirited away from school and now being kept in a boarding school in Smolensk. [So also] Mikhail Khorev, who has 20% vision in one eye only, the legless cripples N. Matiukhina and M. Belan from Tashkent, S. T. Golev, who is an old man and a diabetic and is denied medicine, and many others whom we have not enumerated.

7. DISRUPTION OF FUNERAL SERVICES

V. I. Butenko, who lived at 24 Shimatskaia St, Mirgorod, Poltava Oblast, made a dying request to his wife and son that they bury him as a believer. During the funeral procession the militia intervened, thrust the widow of the deceased aside, and did not give her the body for burial. This happened on 26 March 1967. [From another source it is known that Butenko had been a communist – see *Problems of Communism*, XVII, 4, 1968, p. 102.]

8. FALSE WITNESSES IN COURT

Witnesses who are called by the accused to explain the case are not admitted. But attention is paid to the testimony of citizens who have evoked a protest by relatives of the prisoners about their participation in court. Such as, for example, the participation of militia Major Zudin, who after his deposition at the trial of V. Shuportiak and V. Kozlov publicly called for mass extermination of believers. Nevertheless even after the protest he served as the chief accuser in many trials which took place in Moscow, including the trials of the members of the Council of Churches of the E.C.B., N. G. Baturin, G. K. Kriuchkov and G. P. Vins.

At factory workers' meetings believers endure insults and

abuse by the masses of workers who are incited by the organs of government and shop-stewards, who display hatred to the E.C.B. by calling them obscurantists, lunatics, swindlers, American spies, child sacrificers, thieves of state property and the like.

9. FORCIBLE COMMITMENT OF E.C.B. BELIEVERS TO PSYCHIATRIC HOSPITALS

There are cases in which healthy believers of the E.C.B. are committed to psychiatric hospitals. On 17 October 1966 the believer of the E.C.B. V. P. Kolesnik was on the premises of the C.C. C.P.S.U. for a personal interview with comrade Shelepin on the question of re-establishment of his pension, which had been stopped by order of the secretary of the city Party committee of Sinelnikovo, Dnepropetrovsk Oblast. From the premises of the C.C. he was taken to psychiatric hospital No. 15, Moscow, where an interrogation was made concerning internal church matters.

In Riazan the believer P. Safronov was arrested on 21 June 1966. On 23 September 1966 he was transferred to the Serbskii Institute of Psychiatry in Moscow. We do not know what kind of experiments were conducted on him, nor in what condition we will find him, but we do know that he was healthy when he was arrested. At present he has been condemned to six years' deprivation of freedom, on 13 January 1967, according to the political Article 70 of the Criminal Code of the R.S.F.S.R.

There are other similar cases. [*further sections are here omitted*]

5 June 1967   (signed)
LYDIA P. VINS (Kiev),
NINA P. YAKIMENKOVA (Moscow Region),
ALEKSANDRA T. KOZOREZOVA (Omsk),
KLAVDIYA V. KOZLOVA (Mari A.S.S.R.),
ELIZAVETA A. KHRAPOVA (Tashkent),
(full addresses given).

(Full text in *R.C.D.A.*, New York, VII, 3–4, February 1968, pp. 23–40.)

DOCUMENT 5

IMPRISONMENT OF A SANE PERSON IN A MENTAL HOSPITAL

V. I. Kuznetsova's Letter to Izvestia

[This letter did not appear in *Izvestia*, but was later printed in the Roman paper *Il Popolo*, 17 April 1967. Russian text in *Possev*, 12 May 1967.]

On 13 March 1965 my husband V. V. Kuznetsov spoke at a discussion in Moscow University. His contribution was not to the taste of someone. In the autumn he was twice summoned to the K.G.B. He was warned that a charge under Article 70 of the Criminal Code or a mental hospital lay in wait for him.

And vengeance did strike my husband. To begin with he was thrown out of his job on 26 October 1966 in connexion with the abolition of the post of non-staff artist. 'Abolition of the post of non-staff artist!' My eye! Then on 1 November at 6 a.m. he was grabbed and delivered in a police van, escorted by a policeman and a nurse, to the Moscow Region psychiatric hospital on 8th of March Street. The order said: 'V. V. Kuznetsov, born 1936 and residing at Armand Settlement, house 16, is sent for consultation and diagnosis. Diagnosis No. 300. Doctor Voitsekhovich.'

This was surrounded by violet-coloured official stamps.

Since when have people been picked up for diagnosis so early in the morning?

Since when have people been delivered in police vans for diagnosis?

In the hospital the distracted and astonished doctors did not know what to do. Eventually they decided to telephone (and where to!?) to the chief of the district police in the town of Pushkino.

Since when has the psychiatrist M. Ya. Koltunova been obliged to turn to the district police chief A. M. Deyev in order to ask whether or not to detain a person sent for examination?

Since when have psychiatrists been subordinate to the police?

Moreover, a sheet was attached to the order with the type-written text:

Kuznetsov Victor Vasilyevich. Expresses wild ideas on human interaction and relations. Considers the attitude of his relatives incorrect. Divorced his wife because of a wild interpretation of their mutual relations.

Considers the attitude to him at work to be incorrect. Reacts wildly to the attempts of other people to speak.

Expresses critical views about the government. Criticizes various sorts of government measures. Changes his job in relation to his wild interpretation of the attitude to him at work.

Since when have sheets been attached to orders for diagnosis with such an illiterate and false content?

What is this? This is a diagnosis which has *already* been established, *before the examination.*

Let us read: 'Divorced his wife because of a wild interpretation of their mutual relations.'

I, the wife of V. V. Kuznetsov and mother of two children, declare: *This is a lie!* This is a lie like all the rest. From beginning to end a lie.

I believe that *all this has been inspired by the K.G.B.*, all this is the most enormous mistake, *all this* is a sad *echo* of the period of the cult of personality.

Release my husband!

I beg you to publish my statement.

15 December 1966.   V. I. KUZNETSOVA
                                         Armand Settlement 16,
                                         Pushkino, Moscow region.

(At some stage Kuznetsov must have been released, because it has since been reported that he was arrested on 20 March 1969 after a draft of a new Soviet constitution had been found in his house.)

Conscientious Objection

Patricia May

The extent and limits of the right of conscientious objection are extraordinarily difficult to define. As I suggested in my introductory chapter, the question is connected with the age-old problem of deciding when the citizen may rightly disobey the law, a problem which will no doubt be discussed so long as political philosophy exists.

The central questions are, what limits, if any, may the state set to the citizen's freedom of conscience, and are there any circumstances in which a human being has a right or duty to sacrifice conscience and obey orders which conflict with what conscience enjoins. These questions entail further questions about such matters as the proper relations between Church and State and, at the personal level, about the difficulty of being certain that a conscientious decision has been taken upon full and correct information.

These questions cannot be answered, or even discussed here. Perhaps they can never be definitively answered. But what Mrs May shows in her paper is that some states have begun to formulate answers to some of them, which are humane and yet do not interfere with the essential machinery of government. Her argument is that the example of these states should be followed by the many which retain repressive legislation to deal with those citizens who object on conscientious grounds to military service, or any substitute for it. – C.R.H.

I am accused of the so-called crime of refusing to be inducted into the armed forces, to which I plead guilty; what I have done in fact is to refuse to be inducted into an institution that orders and trains men to kill. James Wilson, U.S.A., 1966.

THE term 'conscientious objector' is applied to those who by reason of their conscience refuse to be involved in war, or, by extension, in military service of any kind. Objection takes a number of different forms; members of many religious sects refuse to be involved in any violence and therefore refuse to fight or be trained for fighting; some refuse only to be involved in any combatant duties but will accept non-combatant duties; others refuse to be connected with military service at all, even to the extent of doing non-combatant work; but instead of military service, accept alternative civilian service; others believe that they must refuse even alternative civilian service, since such an acceptance, to them, means acquiescing in the system of military service.[1]

Objectors are not confined to those who follow the rulings of an organized religion. There are many individuals who, from humanitarian or philosophical principle, believe that armed force is wrong, and are totally opposed to war in general. However, there is another category of objector to which belongs the person who, although he is not a pacifist, refuses to fight in one particular war, or type of war, on the grounds that it is wrong or immoral. The problems of one or another category of conscientious objector have been known in every country which has been at war or where there is or has been compulsory conscription. The last category, the 'selective objector', has however been given more prominence by the Vietnam war and its effect on many young Americans who have been liable for conscription. The claims of this category may not appear to some to have as much merit as those of total objectors to war; nevertheless they are claims of right and cannot be excluded from a general consideration of conscientious objection as a human right.

The right to refuse military service is perhaps not one of the most obvious of human rights, but it is certainly a fundamental one and must be contained in the United Nations Declaration of Human Rights, 1948, since it derives logically from the 'right to freedom of thought, conscience and religion' included in Article 18 of the Declaration. One major problem, however, is that the concept of conscientious objection to military service has never been 'fashionable' even at present when there is a growing apprehension that small-scale fighting leads to war, that small wars lead

---

1. The author is greatly indebted to all those who gave help concerning this paper, and especially to the Society of Jehovah's Witnesses, War Resisters International, the Mennonite Society of London and the Friends' Peace and International Relations Committee.

to bigger wars, and that another full-scale war would mean total annihilation. Perhaps, because aggression is supposed to be a basic human instinct, refusal to fight is felt, consciously or unconsciously, to be not quite normal, or even cowardly. Nevertheless, pacifism is a basic part of the religious or ethical code of many different groups of people and, as will be seen, those who have adhered to their principles have suffered as much as those persecuted for persisting in any other religious, political or ethical belief which is condemned by the state whose authority they have flouted – and have often suffered more than those who have been involved in military service. But because the concept of conscientious objection lacks glamour, those who are persecuted for their refusal to do military service seldom attract the main beam of publicity. Since their 'crime' is a negative one, there is no dramatic demonstration of principle for the world to notice and sympathize with, unlike, for instance, the writers of Russia or the Freedom Fighters of Southern Africa.

Thus, in spite of the efforts of organizations devoted to the cause of pacifism, the plight of those persecuted for holding to their belief in non-violence has largely escaped the concern of the world. Such people are the forgotten dissenters. Their rights are as important as any other rights, but until their problem is brought to the notice of the world there will be a lack of that moral pressure so essential in establishing the recognition of human rights. Once the facts concerning the widespread persecution of so many individuals are known, their cause may provoke the necessary concern, but since so many different groups in so many different countries are involved, it is extremely difficult to initiate any co-ordinated campaign on behalf of conscientious objectors or even to collect information about what is happening to them in countries where their beliefs go unrecognized.

The treatment of conscientious objectors by different states and the discrimination against various categories of conscientious objectors is a complex subject and a comprehensive survey is impossible in the limited space of this paper, which is mainly confined to a study of those conscientious objectors, in a cross-section of states, who are being subjected to abuse and harsh punishments for remaining firm to their principles. Our intention is to spotlight the worst situations, and point out where there is need for further reform in some countries where the provisions for conscientious objectors are so limited as to be almost useless.[2]

It must be emphasized that since information is so widely scattered, only the tip of the iceberg can be seen. The cases which will be mentioned here have in the main been collected by Amnesty with the cooperation of other organizations and religious groups; however, Amnesty is the only organization known by the author to have a library of case-histories of such prisoners of conscience; and Amnesty can only deal with those prisoners who have been brought to its notice either by press references or by other organizations or individuals, and only acts on behalf of those who have agreed to its help.

It will be noticed that a great many case-histories concern Jehovah's Witnesses. This is partly because the Society of Jehovah's Witnesses is extremely efficient in collecting information about what has happened to its members, and partly because, since Jehovah's Witnesses do not accept any form of national service at all, they are more widely penalized than other sects. On the first point some religious groups are afraid that any publicity concerning persecution of their members might lead to further punishment; on the second point, it should be emphasized that there are religious groups who, while officially accepting alternative service where such is provided, leave it to their members' consciences as to whether they will accept this compromise. While no definite case-histories have been put forward, it appears that individuals (particularly among the Society of Friends) have been known to refuse to compromise their religious beliefs by accepting military service or any other form of alternative service. Furthermore, it seems that the total of those serving sentences for refusal to do military service must run into thousands.

The problem of conscientious objection mainly arises in those countries where compulsory military service in time of peace still exists. It should not be forgotten, however, that although the cases mentioned concern conscientious objection to military service, there have been many cases of regular soldiers who become con-

2. War Resisters International *Survey on Conscientious Objection* is to be published in 1969.

scientious objectors and wish to be discharged. However, the incidence of such cases is obviously far less frequent.

Some countries do not recognize the right of conscientious objection to military service at all; others only recognize it to the extent of providing a limited form of non-combatant service. Refusal to do military service, where conscientious objection is not accepted as a right by the state concerned, naturally constitutes a criminal offence and the conscientious objector is punished in the same way as any other criminal. Punishment can take the form of fines or loss of civil rights – which can mean that the conscientious objector will no longer be able to find work in his country. In many cases prison sentences are imposed, often for long periods, and punishments are equivalent to those for serious criminal offences. The conscientious objector seldom receives more rights or privileges than any criminal and is often confined in appalling conditions. Worse still, since in many countries a man continues to be liable for military service until he reaches the age limit for conscription, when a conscientious objector has ended one sentence, he is called up again immediately, and when he again refuses to obey military orders, is re-sentenced. He can thus be punished repeatedly for the same offence. It is impossible to deal with such a problem in general terms, however. To gain an understanding of the scope of the penalties incurred by conscientious objectors, the position in those western European countries where there are no provisions for conscientious objectors will be considered first; then that in communist countries; then the difficulties arising where countries have limited provisions for conscientious objectors; and finally the problems facing selective conscientious objectors, i.e. those who object to certain wars or types of war.

In western Europe, now, the majority of countries recognize to some degree the right to refuse military service. However, there are glaring exceptions, of which one of the most striking in recent years has been the death sentence passed in 1966 on a young Greek conscientious objector, Christos Kanzanis, a Jehovah's Witness. This religious group takes its principles from direct interpretation of the Bible. Its members believe that Christians must keep a strictly neutral position with regard to the affairs of the state. They are opposed to all armed force and therefore to military service or any substituted form, although they play their part in any civilian project unconnected with military service where citizens' aid is required. This viewpoint may be thought extreme, but Witnesses will take the most extreme consequences for these beliefs; indeed thousands of them were put into concentration camps in Hitler's Germany as a result of the courageous stand that they took against Nazism.

In Greece the law provides that every male between the ages of twenty-one and thirty-five is liable to do a period of 18 to 21 months' military service. There is no recognition of the right of conscientious objection and the Constitution expressly excludes the right to refuse on religious grounds.[3] Kanzanis was first called up for service in 1964 and when he refused he was sentenced to a term of imprisonment. At the end of his sentence he was again called up and when he again refused he was sentenced to death, on a charge of refusing to take up a weapon. Fortunately such international protest followed that the sentence was commuted to imprisonment for four and a half years, a sentence which seems very lenient by comparison, until it is pointed out that in Greece any sentence of over five years carries automatic loss of civil rights. Apart from the more unpleasant consequences of such loss, this means that a person is no longer liable for military service. Therefore when Kanzanis ends his term of imprisonment in 1970 there is nothing to prevent his recall for military service and the imposition of another sentence when he refuses.

In March 1968 there were forty-three Jehovah's Witnesses in Greece known to Amnesty who were serving prison sentences as conscientious objectors. Because they are sentenced repeatedly to successive terms of imprisonment, it is common for them to spend twelve years or more in prison. Treatment while in prison depends on the particular prison authorities. Where there is a strong Greek Orthodox influence treatment is harsh since the Church is firmly opposed to the Witnesses, but in other places, since conscientious objectors generally are better-educated than the average prisoner,

3. Art. 2 S.5 of the Constitution: 'Religious convictions cannot be used as grounds for exemption from the fulfilment of obligations to the State or for refusing to uphold the laws of the country.' (This Constitution dates from 1952).

they often receive less arduous tasks such as clerical work. Jehovah's Witnesses do not regard themselves as political prisoners, since their stand is based on their religious beliefs and they are entirely neutral on all political issues.

Kanzanis was not the only man to receive a death sentence. Another Witness, George Roussopoulos, was sentenced to death a few months before Kanzanis, but his sentence was commuted to seven years' imprisonment. This illustrates the great discrepancy in the manner of sentencing conscientious objectors in Greece. One man may receive a five-year sentence, which as mentioned above prevents him from being obliged to do military service again, while another may receive a sentence of four years and ten months, which means that he can be recalled and re-sentenced the moment the last term of imprisonment is served.

The situation is as bad in Spain. Call-up age is twenty-one and liability continues until the age of forty-five. There is no recognition of the right of conscientious objection and all men except Catholic priests are liable for service. In June 1967 a new law was passed concerning religious liberty, and it was hoped that this would provide for exemption of all ministers of religion from military service. Since all Jehovah's Witnesses regard themselves as ministers, the law could have released them from military service. However, right-wing opinion prevailed and when the Act was finally passed it provided that non-Catholic ministers, unlike Catholic priests, would still be liable for military service. Refusal is still a crime, which is committed anew each time a man refuses to obey a military order, and carries a penalty of imprisonment.

As the law stands, conscientious objectors can be given repeated terms of imprisonment indefinitely, since as soon as one term is ended they are again ordered to commence military duties, and are sentenced when they refuse. There are at least sixty-seven Witnesses in prison in Spain, serving sentences ranging from first terms of six months to three years, to multiple terms totalling fourteen years. In fact many face a lifetime in gaol for holding to their beliefs. It seems that the numbers of those given prison sentences increases each year. Of the sixty-seven mentioned above, twenty were serving first sentences. Recent information indicates that another fifty Jehovah's Witnesses are waiting to be sentenced.

The case of twenty-nine-year-old Alberto Contijoch Berenguer has aroused much attention. He has been in prison since 1959 when he was first called up but refused to put on military uniform. Since then he has been released twice, called up again immediately and court-martialled each time for 'wilfully disobeying an order'. After serving his last sentence he was transported to the Spanish Sahara. Cardinal Heenan heard about this case and when he was in Rome in September 1967 for the Bishops' Synod, he took the opportunity of bringing to the attention of the Spanish bishops the failure of their country to provide legal recognition of those who object to military service on religious grounds. It appears that so far the Cardinal's efforts have met with no success.

Although most cases known to Amnesty concern Jehovah's Witnesses, they are of course not the only religious group involved in the struggle of conscientious objectors in Spain. In December 1966 David Duran Gongora, a Seventh Day Adventist, was sentenced to six months' imprisonment. On his release he was immediately put in custody of the military authorities to face a second trial. In February 1968 a report appeared in a Spanish newspaper that Ruben Escribano Esteban, also a member of the Seventh Day Adventists, was sentenced to six years' imprisonment for refusing to obey a command and take up arms on the sabbath. There are also many Quakers in Spain who would be affected but at the date of writing no information is available concerning their treatment.[4]

It is just possible that something may be done to prevent repeated sentences. In a civil case a Spanish court has held that where the offence is a continuing one (in this instance refusal to undergo a medical examination) the defendant could only be punished *once* for such an offence. This precedent will be used to argue the case against the imposition of recurrent sentences on conscientious objectors.

No court martial in Spain has ever acquitted anyone refusing to do military service on grounds of conscience. Although Spain is an officially Catholic country the government has ignored a resolution by the Second Vatican Council urging that 'laws make humane provision for the case of those who, for reasons of conscience, re-

4. A survey by the Society of Friends is in preparation.

fuse to bear arms'. Nevertheless the Vatican pronouncement has been noticed. In August 1967 an editorial in *Ya*, a national newspaper, tried to reconcile the Spanish attitude with the pronouncement. This attempt was scathingly rejected by a well-known Madrid lawyer, Eduardo Cierco Sanchez, in a Catholic magazine, *El Ciervo*. Cierco pointed out how the *Ya* editorial had so loosely interpreted the Vatican Council's text as to make it completely misleading. Much of the pressure to alter the law comes from Spaniards who are not conscientious objectors. This pressure seems to be making itself felt; in April 1968 the Madrid newspaper *ABC* quoted a Señor Lopez, an under-secretary of the Ministry of Justice, as saying that (regarding conscientious objection etc., and compulsory military service) 'an adequate formula is being sought that would reconcile religious liberty with the obligations of all Spaniards. . . . At the moment we are trying to soften the few situations that have been produced.'

Regrettably, the Vatican pronouncement has not yet had much effect even in Italy. By Article 52 of the Italian Constitution the defence of the fatherland is the sacred duty of the citizen and military service is compulsory within the terms set down by the law. Although there are a number of provisions in the Constitution concerning freedom of religion and conscience, decisions of military courts have consistently held that conscientious objection is not recognized by Italian law. Furthermore, the Constituent Assembly has recently overruled a proposal that persons objecting to bearing arms for philosophical or religious reasons should be exempted from doing so.

Since then a law, known as the Legge Pedini, has been introduced and approved in principle, presumably in response to demands for more enlightened action by the Constituent Assembly. This provides that certain suitably qualified conscientious objectors may be permitted to work for a period in an underdeveloped country instead of doing military duties; however, it seems that 'suitably qualified' is being so narrowly interpreted as to benefit very few conscientious objectors. At present, as in Spain, only Catholic priests are exempt. For everyone else the call-up age is twenty and a man's liability for military service continues until he is forty-one. The law imposes severe penalties on conscientious objectors in order to ensure that compulsory service is carried out. The first sentence can range from six months to two years. The offence is viewed objectively: in one case concerning a Catholic conscientious objector, Guiseppe Gozzini, in 1962, the Florence military court refused to accept conscientious objection as a mitigating circumstance when considering Gozzini's penalty for refusal to do military service. Furthermore, in Italy too, a conscientious objector can be called up again and re-sentenced for refusal and in theory this process may continue until he is over call-up age. Of the fifty-two Jehovah's Witnesses at present imprisoned for refusing military service many have served five sentences. Ruggieri Dante, aged twenty-three, has so far been sentenced to a total of fifty months' imprisonment. The practice seems to be that a conscientious objector is ordered to put on military uniform while still in prison at the end of one sentence, and when he refuses he is re-arrested and eventually re-sentenced to another term. This happened to a Jehovah's Witness, Guiseppe Ionata, aged twenty-one, when he had served his second sentence. When he refused to put on uniform he was re-arrested immediately. He is now serving a third sentence, and is only one of many subjected to this treatment.

Conscientious objectors do not receive any special treatment in prison. Conditions in Italian prisons are very bad. In fact many conscientious objectors are eventually discharged before the age-limit for military service because of ill-health – probably due to the bad effects of years spent in these prisons.

It may not be unexpected that under such régimes as those of Greece and Spain there is no recognition of such beliefs as conscientious objection. It is more surprising to find that Switzerland, which has compulsory conscription, does not recognize the rights of conscientious objectors or provide any form of alternative service. Men are liable to perform a period of military service every year while of age for conscription. Under the Swiss Constitution the obligation to perform military service overrides the section guaranteeing freedom of religion and conscience. The only provision for those who are conscientious objectors by reason of religious beliefs is that once registered by the military authorities they may declare themselves to be conscientious objectors and may choose to do non-combatant work in the medical or clerical corps. However, they first have to comply with enlistment procedure. If they refuse to comply they are liable to receive prison sentences ranging from three days to three years, and can be sentenced year after year unless released from liability. But the Constitution does allow the court to substitute a sentence called *arrêts répressifs* for conscientious objectors refusing military service for religious reasons. This means that the prisoner may choose his work while in prison and have certain other privileges, e.g. more visitors. Furthermore, from 1 March 1968 there will be provision for conscientious objectors to work outside prison during the day, at hospitals or in factories – under guard – and to return to the prison at nights and presumably week-ends. In 1965, 100 conscientious objectors refused military service, and it seems that the numbers are increasing.

There are conflicting reports concerning the Swiss authorities' attitude at present. According to one source of information, there is a tendency towards milder treatment. The maximum penalty appears to have been reduced to six months, and many have been released from further liability to perform military service after the first sentence. However, another source, the journal of Internationale de la Résistance à la Guerre, the Swiss section of War Resisters International, reported that in 1966, ninety-nine conscientious objectors were convicted and that sentences for conscientious objectors are now more serious than they were at that time; the first quarterly edition of the journal lists the cases of about twenty conscientious objectors of differing types who have been convicted during the last few months for refusing military service. These include the case of Hans Heiri Zurrer, a pacifist who was at one time a clergyman. He refused military service repeatedly and was eventually discharged from the army and his citizen's rights were withdrawn. In 1959 he applied for a post in the Church. This was refused by the Church Council of the Zürich Canton – mainly, it is believed, on account of his conscientious objection and refusal to obey the laws concerning military service. He is liable to pay a military exemption tax and he has consistently refused to pay this; instead he sends the amount payable each year to various charitable institutions and sends the receipt for these donations to the military authorities, with an offer to pay the same amount to any non-military institutions nominated by the authorities. It appears that this offer has not been accepted and in November 1967 he faced his eighteenth conviction. His sentences each year have ranged from one to three weeks. Another conscientious objector, an anarchist, received his third sentence – of six months' imprisonment. He has so far served eleven months in total and since he was not discharged from further military duty is liable for further recall and thus another conviction.

Another conscientious objector, Hermann Müller, sentenced for the fourth time, to six months' imprisonment, was discharged from further liability but lost his civil rights for a period of two years. It may be that the discrepancy in treatment reflects the different attitude towards those refusing military service for straightforward religious reasons and those objecting on more complicated moral or political grounds.

Fritz Tuller, secretary of the Swiss section of War Resisters International, was sentenced to four months' imprisonment in September 1967 for refusing the yearly service. He refused to attend the Tribunal and he warned the authorities that, at the time he was expected to attend, he would be distributing leaflets in which he stated that he refused to serve in the Swiss army which was 'an army of a country tied economically and spiritually to rich countries which exploit the underdeveloped countries while seeking to conserve and enlarge their privileges by military coups and wars of extermination'. Tuller had spent his last two summers doing voluntary service in Albinen and Montoggio, a fact which he mentioned in his leaflet which recommended others to do likewise. He is now (July 1968) back in prison.

There is some hope that in Europe, at any rate, steps will be taken to improve the lot of conscientious objectors. In September 1965 Amnesty International drew the attention of the Council of Europe, with whom it has consultative status, to the subject of the rights of conscientious objectors, and in May 1966 ten Assembly members of the Council signed a motion recommending that the Committee of Experts on Human Rights should be instructed by the Committee of Ministers of the Council to 'examine the possibility of defining the guiding principles concerning the right of conscientious objectors to abstain from performing military service on grounds of conscience'. (Council of Europe, Consultative Assembly, Doc. 2170.)

The Max Planck Institute was requested by the Legal Committee of the Council to prepare a study of the legal situation of conscientious objectors in the member states of the Council of Europe, and in January 1967 the Legal Committee reported its findings to the Assembly, which adopted (*inter alia*) the resolution that

> Having regard to Article 9 of the European Convention on Human Rights which binds member states to respect the individual's freedom of conscience and religion ... persons liable to conscription for military service who for reasons of conscience or profound conviction arising from religious, ethical, moral, humanitarian, philosophical or similar motives, refuse to perform armed service shall enjoy a personal right to be released from the obligation to perform such service.

The Assembly outlined the procedure to be adopted for registering as a conscientious objector and the rules for alternative service. It recommends, rightly, that conscientious objectors should be dealt with by an administrative organization entirely separate from the military authorities; suggests that alternative service should be at least as long as military service (but gives no limit to the period of military service), and finally recommends 'social and financial equality'. However, these recommendations do not take into consideration the fact that some sects, for instance Jehovah's Witnesses, find it against their beliefs to comply with the suggested procedure for registration or any form of alternative service; neither do they appear to take account of conscientious objectors who have no general objections to fighting but who refuse to fight in certain wars or under certain conditions of service.

Moreover, the recommendations of the Committee of Experts are only applicable to member states of the Council of Europe, and of course there are conscientious objectors in almost every country where there is conscription. In many countries where there is conscription and no provision for conscientious objectors, there is no adequate machinery to enforce enlistment, so no problems have yet arisen, but in communist countries, where there is conscription and a very efficient machinery for enforcement, except to a very limited extent in East Germany (see below), no form of conscientious objection is recognized.

In the U.S.S.R., for instance, the law is based on the total separation of religion and the state, and provides that 'no one may by virtue of his religious outlook decline to fulfil his obligations as a citizen'. The Russian Penal Code of 1926 specifically states: 'religious scruples are no excuse for failure to perform military duties.' In the 1961 Penal Code no actual mention is made of conscientious objection but there are articles dealing with the penalties for avoiding enlistment or military duties. Such offences are punishable by loss of freedom for one to three years. Since religious groups are not allowed to combine it is difficult to get information concerning them. However, it is known that there are religious groups in Russia who are opposed to war. It is estimated that there are about 40,000 Mennonites in Russia; this group 'standing somewhere between the Baptists and the Quakers' (according to the London Mennonite Newsletter of December 1960) are opposed to war, military service and conscription. There are also large numbers of Jehovah's Witnesses as well as other sects with pacifist principles. In 1960 there were press reports concerning four Jehovah's Witnesses who were convicted in Odessa, and three members of a Pentecostal sect who were sentenced to six, five and three years in a forced labour camp. They were not in fact charged on religious grounds but with 'subversive activity against the safety of the state inspired by the imperialist instigators of war'!

It does appear, however, that other conscientious objectors are dealt with administratively. In 1960 there was a report that three members of the Malevanzy sect who were conscientious objectors were examined by the military authorities when called for service; their papers were then returned to them and they were told to go home. It seems that a small number are actually imprisoned for conscientious objections. However, it is very difficult to tell from reports of court proceedings whether the offences charged are those relating to conscientious objection, and it has proved impossible to obtain more definite information.

The situation in East Germany is only slightly better; it seems that there is an extremely limited acknowledgement of conscientious objection. Since January 1962 there has been eighteen months' compulsory military service for men between eighteen and twenty-six years of age. In September 1964 an amendment to the law was introduced, providing for the establishment of construction units under the Ministry of Defence. Thus those who object to military service for religious or similar reasons can be permitted to join a construction unit once they have been recruited, instead of performing armed service. However, these *Bausoldaten* have to wear military uniform and to take an oath of loyalty 'to work efficiently for the army and to defend the Socialist states against the enemy and to guard all military and state secrets'. They are supervised by regular officers and in fact are soldiers without arms. This type of service is not acceptable to certain groups of conscientious objectors. There were in March 1968 154 Jehovah's Witnesses serving prison sentences of an average term of twenty months. Of these, five were serving a second sentence. They are mainly in forced labour camps, working in copper mills, mines and on the railways. Apart from Jehovah's Witnesses there are others who object to the form of alternative service offered, and it is understood that there have been other prison sentences passed on other kinds of conscientious objectors.

One such case is that of Werner Wiedler, a Lutheran. In 1966, at the age of twenty-two, he was sentenced to three years' imprisonment for conscientious objection. The construction units themselves have not been trouble-free. In 1965 it was reported that a unit of conscientious objectors was ordered to work at a military air base. Twelve refused to do so and eventually five of their number were imprisoned for six months.

However, the attitude of the East German authorities is progressive compared to other communist countries. In particular the situation in Yugoslavia is shocking. Yugoslavia does not recognize the right of conscientious objection and has no provisions at all even for conscientious objectors to perform noncombatant duties while on military service. Conscientious objectors are usually tried by court martial, whose proceedings are not reported in the press.

The conscientious objectors here are mainly members of the Nazarene sect, a religious group who refuse to take up arms, deriving their principles from the Gospel precept 'love thine enemy'. There are about 15,000 Nazarenes in Yugoslavia, about 80% of whom are farmers. They live very quietly and take little part in public life. The individual congregations administer themselves and there is no elaborate superstructure linking the congregations to a central organization. Nazarenes have a simple, perhaps naïve attitude; they accept the authority of the government ruling their country since they believe that all governmental power has some kind of divine sanction. The only conflicts with the government concern the taking of oaths, since they will not swear, and military laws. They accept conscription and refuse only to take up arms. They believe that they should endure any sort of persecution rather than compromise their Christian principles. And certainly the penalties inflicted on them have been among the worst imposed on conscientious objectors anywhere.

In 1960 Jan Stefanides, a Nazarene aged twenty, was sentenced to nine years in solitary confinement for refusing to accept a weapon. The court 'rejected as without foundation' the defence that Stefanides' religious principles forbade him to accept a weapon, stating that although freedom of religion was granted to every citizen, such dogmas if acting in contradiction with any positive laws of the state cannot be justified by religious obligation. His sentence was so harsh because his conduct was 'very damaging to the community'.

In 1965 War Resisters International reported that about six young Nazarenes were being sentenced each year for refusal to carry weapons, to terms of imprisonment up to ten years. Some were receiving second and third sentences up to the age limit for service, thirty years. Nine young men were known to be serving sentences on Goli Otok, a prison on a barren island in the Adriatic. Among them were Dejan Jevremov, sentenced to ten years' imprisonment in 1963 for an offence described by his father as 'his refusal to carry arms and his belief in God'. Conditions in Goli Otok were extremely severe. An ex-prisoner, when interviewed in 1965, said that prisoners were mainly employed in quarries working on the cutting and refining of stone. The food rations provided

no more than bare subsistence, inadequate to maintain good
health since prisoners were worked to the point of exhaustion.
Nazarenes received ill-treatment when they refused to work on
Sundays. They were put in solitary confinement in tiny cells and
their rations were halved. Although it was forbidden to attack
prisoners, beatings did occur frequently. Relatives were only
allowed visits three or four times a year. All this was endured as a
result of adhering strictly to the commandment 'Thou shalt not
kill'.

Certainly these young Nazarenes have proved, by what they
have been willing to endure, the sincerity of their beliefs. Over
recent years Amnesty International and the War Resisters International have made strong representations to the Yugoslav
Government expressing concern for the Nazarene conscientious
objectors. Whether coincidentally or not, there has been a marked
improvement in their treatment. All conscientious objectors are
now released after serving five years, and it appears that they will
no longer be liable for further sentences. Conditions in prison
have improved and relatives are able to visit more freely. However,
there still do not seem to be any provisions for Nazarenes to serve
in non-combatant posts while performing military service.

While no details are available it appears that there are also
Nazarenes serving sentences for refusal to do military service in
Hungary. In Czechoslovakia, also, it is estimated that there are
about twenty Jehovah's Witnesses and Seventh Day Adventists in
prison.

So far we have only considered countries which have no provisions for exemption from military service for conscientious
objectors. Until recently France was in this category: military
service was compulsory for all able-bodied men of twenty and
over and all conscientious objectors were automatically given
prison sentences by military tribunals, of about thirty months'
average, the maximum penalty being five years. In 1963, in response to much pressure, a new Act was passed guaranteeing the
rights of conscientious objectors; this law provides that all will
continue to be called up but those who have declared themselves before enlistment to be conscientious objectors on religious or philosophic grounds and who are accepted as such by

the authorities, are given non-combatant duties or sent to a civilian organization to do work in the national interest. However, there are still penalties for those conscientious objectors who refuse to accept this procedure.

These new provisions make no difference to the problems concerning, for example, Jehovah's Witnesses who will not accept any form of alternative service. And since the new laws for conscientious objectors have been in force, it is reported that Jehovah's Witnesses are being treated more severely. There are between one and two hundred in prison at the present time. They usually receive two consecutive terms of imprisonment, normally one plus one or two plus two years. They are now treated as ordinary criminal offenders and are given no privileges.

Not only Jehovah's Witnesses are serving prison sentences in France for conscientious objection. A case which should be mentioned briefly is that of Georges Pinet, a Paris lawyer. He returned his call-up papers and in 1967 was sentenced to four months' imprisonment in Fresnes Prison. His objection as a Christian was based on the use of nuclear weapons, which is not accepted in France, being a selective conscientious objection.

In many other countries, including Sweden, Norway, West Germany and the U.S.A., where there are provisions for alternative service, failure to comply with the regulations concerning registration and alternative employment is an offence, usually punishable by imprisonment. Apart from those belonging to certain sects which decree non-compliance with the procedure for registering as conscientious objectors, there are individuals whose beliefs prevent them from cooperating with the authorities. One such case is that of James Wilson, a member of the Catholic Worker Movement in the U.S.A., who was charged in 1966 with refusal to report for induction into the army. He had burned his draft card at an anti-Vietnam rally in 1965. He stated, ' I stand as a man who believes in total and complete non-violence as taught by Christ' and he went on, in the words which stand at the beginning of this paper, ' I am accused of the so-called crime of refusing to be inducted into the armed forces, to which I plead guilty; what I have done in fact is to refuse to be inducted into an institution that orders and trains men to kill.' He said that he had not applied for conscientious objector status since he could not cooperate in any way with the system and remain a good Christian. 'I would point out at a time like this, when the racial situation is in an uproar and there are riots in the streets and politicians deploring violence, that the people who believe in non-violence are being put behind bars.' He concluded by saying that he was not a 'draft-dodger' and if he had been, he would not have been on trial, since he could have registered as a conscientious objector and avoided military service on religious grounds, that he had broken what was an immoral law, that he would die for anyone in the room but refused to kill. The judge – who was obviously a perceptive and intelligent man – said that Wilson had a great passion for humanity; 'he was not concerned to make a myth of martyrdom.' Wilson was given a sentence of two years' probation. He was fortunate. It was reported in July 1967 that 'dozens of Jehovah's Witnesses' were convicted and received sentences ranging from one year to the maximum of five years in Tulsa, Oklahoma, for draft violations.

The greatest problem concerning conscientious objectors in the U.S.A. at the moment, however, is that which has been dramatically brought to light by the Vietnam war. Hundreds of young Americans opposed to the continuance of the war in Vietnam have refused to be drafted for military service. The law provides for exemption from military service for anyone who 'by reason of religious training and belief is conscientiously opposed to the participation in war *in any form*' (section 6 (j). Military Service Selection Act, 1967). This excludes the selective objector, who opposes a particular war or type of war. In 1967, 952 people were convicted for draft violations. This was the largest number in any year since the Second World War. Offences ranged from failure to cooperate with the draft board and failure to report for induction, to non-possession of a draft card. Furthermore, statistics showed that longer sentences were given to offenders than in previous years. The maximum sentence is five years and the maximum fine, $10,000. However, this has not deterred many from disobeying military orders. In July 1965 three students, David Samas, Dennis Mora and James Johnson, stationed at Fort Hood, Texas, were ordered to board a plane bound for Vietnam. They refused. Before their posting to Fort Hood they had held a press conference to broadcast their intention to refuse to go to Vietnam, and had also filed a suit in the Federal Court challenging the legality of the Vietnam war on the grounds that it violated the Kellogg-Briand treaty and went against the principles cited in the Geneva Accords, 1954, the U.N. Charter, the Nuremberg Judgements and the U.S. Constitution. Their civil case was dismissed and they were arrested by the military authorities before the appeal was heard. They were tried and Samas and Johnson were sentenced to five years' hard labour, while Mora was sentenced to three years' hard labour.

The heaviest sentence since World War I was passed in October 1967 on Clifton Haywood, a Black Muslim, for two offences concerning draft evasion. He was sentenced to two consecutive five-year sentences, making ten years in all, and a $20,000 fine.[5] One may question whether the legislation, in providing that five years should be the maximum penalty, meant that courts could exceed the maximum sentence by imposing consecutive sentences on more than one count relating to the same offence.[6]

In assessing the sincerity of the average draft resister it may be argued that they are better off to receive a prison sentence than to go to Vietnam. But if 'draft-dodging' were their motive then many could have taken the easy way out by registering as conscientious objectors and claiming alternative service. It is, of course, equally true that many objectors would not gain exemption from military service since their reasons are based on objection to one war as opposed to war in general. The case of one particular person in this category which has aroused great interest is that of Captain Brett Levy. Captain Levy entered military service on a plan which allows doctors to finish their training in the army before being drafted. He had hitherto lived in a conventional Jewish middle-class atmosphere, but his attitude towards life, it appears, underwent a profound change when during his medical training he was sent to Bellevue, a public city institution where he came into close contact with destitution and squalor. He was commissioned as a

5. The appeal against sentence is pending.
6. This is of course a very general point which was widely made after the trial of George Blake, the British official who was convicted of spying for the U.S.S.R.

Captain but in fact given no basic military training. He was put in charge of the dermatology clinic at Fort Jackson where he was expected to train Special Forces aidmen in the basic treatment of skin diseases for use in Vietnam. At the time he entered the army he was very concerned about the war and this concern grew while he was at Fort Jackson. He finally decided that he could not in all conscience train people going to fight in Vietnam, and felt that with only the scant knowledge he was able to give them of treatment they might do more harm than good. So he stopped. This was brought to the attention of his superiors, together with other facts about him; that he had been making anti-war statements and that he was active in many civil rights organizations. He was issued with a formal order to train Special Forces aidmen and when he refused, was court-martialled. He was sentenced to three years' imprisonment with hard labour. This man would in all likelihood never have been sent on active service, but he made his stand and received his punishment for conscientious beliefs, not as an objector in the more conventional sense, but because he had a moral objection to participating in a war which he felt to be unjust. Levy's counsel had cited in defence the Nuremberg doctrine that it is a soldier's duty to refuse orders which will result in crimes against humanity. The court allowed this in evidence; in fact it marked the first occasion that an international ruling was accepted in an American court, but the defence failed to prove any consistent policy of war crimes.

It is not suggested that the dilemma concerning conscientious objection to certain wars is an easy one for governments to resolve. Their authority is obviously being threatened by the selective objector much more than by the total objector, who is seen as somehow 'above' politics. However, the selective objector may be just as sincere in his beliefs as the total objector, and his offence merely one of conscience. If the test were subjective, the overriding factor being the sincerity of the belief, then this problem might be solved. For in adopting such a procedure a government would be seen to be making a concession without thereby admitting any impairment of its authority.

Applications for exemption on selective – including political – grounds were certainly accepted in the United Kingdom during the war,[7] notably in the case of an Italian, Caesarei, who objected to fighting in the last stages of the war on the grounds that he might have to fire on his own relatives in the Italian army. The question of refusal to do military service on political grounds was considered by the court in another case, where it came to the conclusion that it must adopt a subjective test and find in favour of the individual if it were proved that he sincerely felt that the war was an unjust one. The fairly severe test was that 'the objection was so deeply held that it became a matter of inner conviction as to right and wrong and not merely an opinion'.[8]

In Australia, where compulsory military service is by ballot of all males aged between twenty and twenty-six, the law allows exemption to the conscientious objector 'whose beliefs do not allow him to engage in any form of military service'. One objector, David Monahan, was recently granted exemption on the grounds that he was opposed to western intervention in the Vietnam war, although he would be prepared to fight if Australia were attacked. Thus, here too, political grounds are accepted.

But of course not every claim to exemption is allowed. Moreover, it seems that the treatment of those who are not exempted is not all that it might be. A letter in the *Guardian* (May 1968) from Melbourne mentions the case of Simon Townsend, a twenty-two-year-old journalist from Sydney, whose application for exemption from military service was rejected. He was duly drafted and re-refused to obey a military order. He was then placed in solitary confinement for twenty-eight days on a bread-and-water diet. He was awakened every half hour throughout the day and night by military police. An army minister, Mr Lynch, when challenged about this treatment, confirmed it and explained that the purpose was 'to check he has not escaped and is still fit and well'!

There are already regulations to ensure compliance with draft procedure. For instance, it is an offence for any person to employ for more than seven days a person who is required to register under the relevant statute and has not registered, or a person who has been called up for service and has failed to comply. However, new legislation is proposed to prevent evasion of military service by

7. There is no longer compulsory military service in the United Kingdom.
8. Dennis Hayes, *Challenge of Conscience*, Allen & Unwin, 1949, p. 64.

those who do not register or who leave the country before call-up is due. The proposed Act will, *inter alia*, give the authorities power to search lists of employees of firms etc., to ascertain those of call-up age, and will 'fine air-lines issuing tickets to those of call-up age or parents who do not inform' (about their sons leaving the country, it is supposed).

Obviously a complete solution would only be possible in some Utopia where there was no war. The problem is mainly dormant in those countries, like England, which have abolished military service, though it exists for those who become conscientious objectors whilst serving in the regular army. Even if all countries abolished compulsory military service in peace-time there would doubtless still be wars, necessitating conscription, and the problem would therefore arise in this context.

Wherever countries try to make arrangements for conscientious objectors they will find the greatest difficulties in respect of those people who not only refuse military service but refuse to cooperate in any schemes for alternative service.

This problem was recently discussed in a Swedish parliamentary debate concerning Jehovah's Witnesses, when a realistic attitude was taken. (Swed. Parl. Debate Nos. 72 and 80, 1966). In Sweden there are provisions for conscientious objectors to perform alternative service. Obviously Jehovah's Witnesses did not comply with the provisions and they were continually sentenced to terms of imprisonment. The Swedish Government was unhappy about this and a committee was set up to investigate the problem and make proposals for a solution. The committee found that in no country could Jehovah's Witnesses be persuaded to perform any kind of service no matter what the consequences. It was therefore proposed that they should be exempt from military service and should not be called upon to perform it. The committee did not feel that thousands of people would become Jehovah's Witnesses in order to escape service, since all intending members were subjected to a stringent examination as to their convictions before being accepted by the sect. This proposal was accepted and Swedish Jehovah's Witnesses are no longer called up.

It is not to be expected that such an enlightened view will be generally adopted. However, the aim of humanitarian organizations should be to persuade all countries to recognize the right of conscientious objection and to allow total exemption; failing that, to make provision for alternative service; to deal humanely with those conscientious objectors who cannot, because of their convictions, comply with any form of alternative service; to release all conscientious objectors imprisoned for their beliefs; failing that, to ensure that long sentences and recurrent sentences are not imposed for such 'crimes of conscience', and to alleviate their conditions while in prison.

Where provisions are made for alternative service, periods of alternative service should not be longer than the period of military service; the status of those doing military service and alternative service should be treated as equal, both socially and financially – and it should be borne in mind that a soldier is fed and clothed by the army whereas a man on civilian service may have to provide his own keep. Finally, conscientious objectors should be dealt with by a civilian board, not by the military authorities.

One may expect to encounter the argument that if conscientious objectors are recognized there will be overwhelming numbers of young men liable for military service who, in good faith or not, will apply for exemption and thus undermine their country's military arrangements. The answer to this is twofold; first, the election procedure should be such as to ensure the sincerity of those who are exempted from military service and the genuine conscientious objector should not be penalized on account of the few who may try to 'dodge' military service purely for their own convenience; second, statistics show that in all countries where there is provision for exemption, only a small minority do apply. In Belgium forty-three cases were reported in 1962, and the official report commented that the number was 'hardly significant'. In 1965, in Germany 0·88% of those called up applied for exemption. In Norway in 1966 there were 28,000 conscripts, 411 conscientious objectors; in 1967, 26,850 conscripts, 576 conscientious objectors – but of this number nearly 100 were not exempted since they were political conscientious objectors, and as such not recognized in Norway. In Sweden in 1964 it was reported that 0·859% of those liable were granted exemption from military service. It seems from these examples that no country need fear that in recognizing conscientious objectors it will lose its army!

This paper has attempted to show that the problem of conscientious objection is not different in kind from the problems facing any citizen who finds some aspect of the law repugnant to his conscience, but that the punishment of this type of nonconformer is often out of all proportion to the 'offence'. Clearly, conscientious objectors also pose problems for governments, for if states are to function at all the citizen must accept that not all governmental decisions will be to his liking. But this does not mean that governments need fear nonconformity, nor punish the harmless minority who, on good grounds of conscience, fail to conform.

International Action for the Protection of Human Rights

Hilary Cartwright

The earlier papers in this book have discussed some philosophical problems about human rights, and given examples of ways in which they are denied. In this final paper Miss Cartwright describes international action and agencies (still in their infancy) for the protection of rights.

The view underlying her argument is that human nature does not improve spontaneously and governments cannot be relied upon to treat their subjects justly unless pressure is brought to bear upon them.

Sometimes public opinion within a country is strong and free enough to prevent abuses, though even in such circumstances outside support is welcome. Furthermore, it is clear that any government, however responsive to democratic pressures, will feel additionally constrained to respect human rights if it has bound itself to do so by the acceptance of some international instrument. The need for some kind of international legal control is of course even greater, and correspondingly difficult to achieve, in countries whose governments are not open to popular pressure.

Miss Cartwright has brought together the details of what has been done so far and makes recommendations for further action. Her paper makes it possible to close on a note of hope a volume in which much has necessarily been gloomy. – C.R.H.

THE other essays of this book are concerned with particular governmental methods of dealing with dissent, which involve the violation of the fundamental rights and freedoms of the dissenting individual. In this essay it is proposed to describe the efforts that ensure that individual human rights are respected and protected by governments, and where necessary to provide some form of international protection. A full study of work in this field is beyond the scope of a book of this nature; this chapter is therefore confined to action for the protection of human rights generally, and to specific action in relation to the rights of freedom of conscience and religion, and freedom of opinion and expression – the rights directly violated when dissent is suppressed.

While there was some international action in the human rights field before the Second World War – for example in the abolition of slavery and the slave trade, for the protection of the individual in war-time, for the protection of the religious or national minorities which came into existence as a result of the redrawing of the boundaries of Europe after the First World War, and for the protection of refugees – it is only since 1945 that human rights generally have been recognized and accepted as a matter of international concern, and that coordinated and planned action has been undertaken with a view to providing international protection.

There are two views about the role that international organs can play in the human rights field. The first, traditional and conservative, view is that human rights are essentially an internal, domestic matter and that international activity should be confined to encouraging and assisting states to provide effective protection of human rights at the national level. The second view, which in the last twenty years has been gaining more and more acceptance, is that human rights are essentially a matter of international concern and that in the world as it is today their effective protection cannot be safely left to individual governments: some form of international protection and control is therefore essential.

As the rest of this chapter will illustrate, the first view has tended to dominate United Nations action in the human rights field, so that it is only in the last few years that the first tentative steps have been taken at the United Nations level to institute the first organs providing some form of international protection.

At the regional level, on the other hand, both the Council of Europe – grouping most of the states of western Europe – and the Organization of American States – grouping most of the states of the American continent – have recognized and accepted the need for international machinery for the protection of human rights. The measures they have adopted are described later in this chapter.

1. THE UNITED NATIONS

THE U.N. CHARTER

The concern of the United Nations with human rights is expressed at the very outset in the Preamble to the Charter: 'We, the people of the United Nations, determined . . . to reaffirm faith in fundamental human rights, in the dignity and worth of the human person, the equal rights of men and women and of nations large and small. . . .' This determination is reflected in a number of subsequent provisions of the Charter. In particular, Article 1 lays down as one of the purposes of the United Nations:

To achieve international cooperation in solving international problems of an economic, social, cultural or humanitarian character, and in promoting and encouraging respect for human rights and for fundamental freedoms for all without distinction as to race, sex, language or religion.

Article 55 of the Charter goes further and provides that the United Nations *shall* promote, among other things: 'Universal respect for, and observance of, human rights and fundamental freedoms for all without distinction as to race, sex, language or religion' and by Article 56 all member states pledge themselves to take joint and separate action in cooperation with the United Nations Organization for the achievement of this and other purposes.

The United Nations Charter is the first international instrument to contain human rights provisions of a general and universally applicable character, and thus marks the first recognition of their international significance. It takes the view that international peace – which is the essential purpose of the United Nations – cannot be maintained if individual human rights are not respected, and thus places the promotion of human rights among the purposes of the Organization.

ORGANS OF THE UNITED NATIONS

The basic structure of the United Nations, with its two principal organs, the Security Council and the General Assembly, is well known. There are, however, a considerable number of other bodies which have been set up over the years, and it is principally these subordinate bodies which have been concerned with human rights questions.

The *Security Council*'s primary responsibility is for the maintenance of international peace and security, so that it is not directly concerned with questions relating to human rights and would only be called upon to act if a human rights issue amounted to a threat to peace or led to a breach of the peace or an act of aggression – in which case it would have power to take action to enforce the peace – or if a dispute arose between states on a human rights issue, the continuance of which was likely to endanger the maintenance of international peace and security, in which case it would have power to ensure by appropriate means that a settlement were reached. In such situations the power of veto of the permanent members of the Security Council (China, France, U.K., U.S.A. and U.S.S.R.) renders effective action difficult on any controversial subject.

It is the *General Assembly* which is the body primarily reponsible for human rights. Article 13 of the Charter requires it to 'Initiate studies and make recommendations for the purpose of ... assisting in the realization of human rights and fundamental freedoms for all without distinction as to race, sex, language or religion.' While the General Assembly is thus the ultimate authority on questions relating to human rights, and can alone adopt conventions and make recommendations to states, responsibility for detailed work in the field – culminating in the preparation of proposals and recommendations for action by the General Assembly – is delegated to subordinate bodies.

The Charter provides for the establishment of an *Economic and Social Council,* consisting of twenty-seven member states elected by the General Assembly. While ECOSOC – as it is generally called – is empowered by Article 62 to 'make recommendations for the purpose of promoting respect for, and observance of, human rights and fundamental freedoms for all' and to 'prepare draft conventions for submission to the General Assembly, with respect to matters falling within its competence', it is also required to set up a commission for the promotion of human rights, and it is in fact this body, the Human Rights Commission, and its subsidiary body, the Sub-Commission on the Prevention of Discrimination and the Protection of Minorities, which do most of the substantive work on human rights projects. ECOSOC itself does little more than act as a forwarding agent to present the results of the work of these two bodies to the General Assembly.

The *Human Rights Commission*, which consists of thirty-two members elected by ECOSOC for a three-year term, meets annually for a period of five or six weeks. When it was established in 1946 it was directed by the Economic and Social Council to prepare and submit proposals, recommendations and reports regarding the following subjects:

(*a*) an international Bill of Rights;
(*b*) international declarations or conventions on civil liberties, the status of women, freedom of information and similar matters;
(*c*) the protection of minorities;
(*d*) the prevention of discrimination on grounds of race, sex, language or religion.

The progress made in these fields will be described in the succeeding sections of this chapter. It is important at this stage, however, to underline that the Commission has not been empowered to investigate or pass judgement upon individual cases of alleged violations of human rights or to take action in specific cases or in relation to specific countries. Its work has been confined to making studies and recommendations, submitting proposals and preparing instruments of a general character.

In order to deal with the last two subjects which had been entrusted to it, the Commission in 1947 set up the *Sub-Commission on the Prevention of Discrimination and the Protection of Minorities* to undertake studies and make recommendations in these two fields. Unlike ECOSOC and the Human Rights Commission, the Sub-Commission does not consist of representatives of governments but of individuals elected in their personal capacity – eighteen in all – and is thus less of a government body than is usual in United Nations organs. It meets once a year for a period of three weeks.

A number of other United Nations bodies also deal with certain aspects of human rights. Since they are not directly concerned with the specific rights to which this book is devoted, it is not proposed to describe them in any detail. They include the Commission on the Status of Women, established by E C O S O C, the Trusteeship Council, established by the Charter itself to watch over non-self-governing territories and the interests of their populations, the Special Committee on the Implementation of the Declaration with regard to the Granting of Independence to Colonial Countries and Peoples, the Special Committee on the Policies of Apartheid of the Government of the Republic of South Africa, both established by the General Assembly, and the High Commissioner for Refugees, who is concerned with all aspects of the problems of refugees.

Within the Secretariat of the United Nations a *Human Rights Division* has been established, under a Director of Human Rights, with continuing responsibility for questions concerning human rights. The Division provides services and documentation relating to human rights to the various organs of the United Nations. It also prepares publications on human rights and administers the advisory services in the human rights field which will be described in due course.

METHODS OF WORK AND ACHIEVEMENTS

As will be clear from this brief outline of the powers of the various U.N. bodies concerned with human rights, the United Nations is not itself in a position to provide protection against violations of human rights. It has none the less been able to undertake a considerable volume and variety of work for the promotion and protection of human rights and fundamental freedoms. The promotion of human rights requires first of all the spread of a knowledge and understanding of what is meant by the concept, both among governments who are ultimately responsible for ensuring that human rights are respected, and among individual citizens for whose benefit these rights have been proclaimed. In this field, the United Nations has considerable achievements to its credit: it has defined and studied in detail the content of specific rights; it has promoted their general acceptance throughout the world, and greatly contributed to educating and informing world opinion. In the field of protection, progress has inevitably been slower, for governments are reluctant to allow what they often regard as outside interference, and in the present state of the world it is upon governments that the effective protection of human rights ultimately depends. None the less, the United Nations has been responsible for the adoption of a growing number of international conventions which require governments to provide adequate protection of certain rights, and has recently taken the first steps towards the establishment of international machinery which may be brought into action if human rights are violated and no effective remedy is provided at the national level. The achievements in these fields will be examined in this section, with particular reference to the two rights with which this book is principally concerned.

The Universal Declaration of Human Rights

The Universal Declaration of Human Rights was adopted by the General Assembly of the United Nations on 10 December 1948. The text had been prepared by the Human Rights Commission as the first element in the international Bill of Rights it had been called upon to prepare and it was adopted substantially in the form submitted by that body, without dissenting vote and with eight abstentions.[1] In form, it was a resolution of the General Assembly and as such had no binding or compulsory force. None the less, its influence and its importance have been incalculable. It has been described as the Charter of Liberty of the oppressed and downtrodden. It sets out the limits which the almighty state machine should not transgress in its dealings with those whom it rules.

While it was adopted as 'a common standard of achievement for all peoples', it has become much more. It has become the yardstick by which all measures, all activities, in the human rights field are assessed. Many of its provisions have been embodied in national constitutions and have been used for purposes of judicial interpretation in different jurisdictions. It has received repeated confirmation in numerous international conventions. Indeed no

1. Albania, Bulgaria, Czechoslovakia, Hungary, Poland, Rumania, South Africa, U.S.S.R.

resolution or convention of the United Nations on a subject dealt with in the Universal Declaration is drafted without a reference in the preamble to the relevant provisions of the Universal Declaration, and its provisions have been used as the guiding principle in innumerable cases by the various organs of the United Nations as well as by other international bodies.

So great has been the impact of the Universal Declaration, and so general its acceptance, that the view is being more and more frequently expressed that its provisions now form part of international customary law, which consists of the 'general principles of law recognized by civilized nations' and which forms part of the body of international law. Such a development would open the way to its being directly applicable in the courts.

Freedom of opinion and expression and freedom of conscience and religion are dealt with in Articles 18 and 19 of the Universal Declaration. They are as follows:

18. Everyone has the right to freedom of thought, conscience and religion; this right includes freedom to change his religion or belief, and freedom, either alone or in community with others and in public or private, to manifest his religion or belief in teaching, practice, worship and observance.
19. Everyone has the right to freedom of opinion and expression; this right includes freedom to hold opinions without interference and to seek, receive and impart information and ideas through any media and regardless of frontiers.

These two provisions have formed the point of departure for all subsequent United Nations work in these fields.

The International Covenants on Human Rights

At the time the Universal Declaration was drawn up, it was decided that it would be followed by one or more international conventions[2] for the protection of the rights and freedoms set forth. Work on these conventions was protracted, and it was not until December 1966 that the International Covenant on

2. Unlike a convention, a declaration does not itself create directly binding obligations. The provisions of a convention, however, are legally binding upon those states which have ratified it. There is no difference between a covenant and a convention.

Economic, Social and Cultural Rights and the International Covenant on Civil and Political Rights, together with an optional protocol to the latter, were finally adopted – though they have not yet been ratified by enough States to become binding. These two Covenants protect in some detail almost all the rights and freedoms contained in the Universal Declaration – including in particular freedom of conscience and religion, and freedom of opinion and expression[3] – together with some others that are not mentioned there (in particular the right to self-determination), and go some way to providing machinery to ensure the implementation of their provisions by those states which ratify them.

In view of the special character of the economic, social and cultural rights – which can be said to constitute a programme of social action rather than a series of immediately enforceable rights – the implementation machinery for those rights consists essentially of a system of reporting by governments to the United

---

3 .The provisions of the Covenant are somewhat more detailed than those of the Universal Declaration; they are as follows:

Article 18

1. Everyone shall have the right to freedom of thought, conscience and religion. This right shall include freedom to have or to adopt a religion or belief of his choice, and freedom, either individually or in community with others and in public or private, to manifest his religion or belief in worship, observance, practice and teaching.
2. No one shall be subject to coercion which would impair his freedom to have or to adopt a religion or belief of his choice.
3. Freedom to manifest one's religion or beliefs may be subject only to such limitations as are prescribed by law and are necessary to protect public safety, order, health, or morals or the fundamental rights and freedoms of others.
4. The State Parties to the present Covenant undertake to have respect for the liberty of parents and, when applicable, legal guardians to ensure the religious and moral education of their children in conformity with their own convictions.

Article 19

1. Everyone shall have the right to hold opinions without interference.
2. Everyone shall have the right to freedom of expression: this right shall include freedom to seek, receive and impart information and ideas of all kinds, regardless of frontiers, either orally, in writing or in print, in the form of art, or through any other media of his choice.
3. The exercise of the rights provided for in paragraph 2 of this article carries with it special duties and responsibilities. It may therefore be subject to certain restrictions, but these shall only be such as are provided by law and are necessary:
    (a) For respect of the rights or reputations of others;
    (b) For the protection of national security or of public order (*ordre public*), or of public health or morals.

Nations on their progress in implementing the Covenant, together with provisions for advice and assistance from the United Nations and its specialized agencies to assist governments in overcoming difficulties and solving problems.

The implementation machinery for civil and political rights goes somewhat further. Provision is made for the establishment of a Human Rights Committee consisting of eighteen members elected for a period of four years by the states parties to the Covenant from candidates proposed by those same states. The primary function of the Committee is to receive and examine reports submitted by states parties to the Covenant on the measures they have adopted to give effect to the rights protected by the Covenant. The Committee's powers in connexion with these reports are limited to transmitting its comments on them to the states concerned and to the Economic and Social Council.

A second stage of implementation machinery comes into force under Article 41 of the Covenant only if a state expressly declares that it accepts the provisions of that Article. Once such a declaration has been made by a particular state, other states parties to the Covenant may make 'Communications' (or complaints) to the Committee alleging that that state is not fulfilling its obligations under the Covenant. Once such a communication has been made, the powers of the Committee in dealing with it are in effect confined to attempting to bring about 'a friendly solution of the matter on the basis of respect for human rights and fundamental freedoms as recognized in the present Covenant'. If the Committee cannot do so itself, it may with the consent of the states concerned appoint an *ad hoc* Conciliation Commission which in its turn attempts to reach an amicable solution. If it is unable to do so, it can do no more than report to the Chairman of the Human Rights Committee. The reports of both the Human Rights Committee and of the Conciliation Commission, if one has been appointed, are communicated only to the states parties concerned.

The most significant form of implementation machinery is provided for in the Optional Protocol to the Covenant, which does not form part of the Covenant itself and requires separate ratification. Under its terms a state which becomes a party of Protocol 'recognizes the competence of the Committee to receive and consider communications from individuals subject to its jurisdiction who claim to be victims of a violation by that State Party of any of the rights set forth in the Covenant'. Thus for the first time the individual is given a right to take a complaint of a violation of his fundamental rights before an organ of the United Nations.[4] Unfortunately the powers of the Committee in dealing with an individual communication are very limited. It can do no more than require the state against whom the complaint has been made to submit a written statement clarifying the matter and the remedy, if any, that may have been taken and thereafter 'forward its views to the State Party concerned and to the individual'.

Other International Conventions

At the same time as work was proceeding on the international Covenants, the United Nations and its specialized agencies were active in securing the preparation and adoption of a considerable number of other conventions dealing with specific rights in some detail. Conventions adopted under the auspices of the United Nations include a Convention on the Prevention and Punishment of the Crime of Genocide (1949); a Supplementary Convention on the Abolition of Slavery, the Slave Trade and Institutions and Practices similar to Slavery (1956 – the original Slavery Convention dates from 1926); a Convention on the Elimination of all forms of Racial Discrimination (1965). The International Labour Organization has been responsible for the adoption of Conventions on the Abolition of Forced Labour; on Freedom of Association and Protection of the Right to Organize; on Equal Remuneration; and on Employment Policy. The High Commissioner for Refugees has secured the passage of Conventions on the Reduction of Statelessness; the Status of Stateless Persons; and the Status of Refugees. In the cultural field, Unesco sponsored a Convention against Discrimination in Education.

In the specific fields of freedom of conscience and religion, and freedom of opinion and expression two draft Conventions have

4. The only exception hitherto had been in relation to territories placed under U.N. Trusteeship or remaining under a League of Nations Mandate, who have a special right of petition under the U.N. Charter.

been prepared but have not yet been adopted. The first is a draft Convention on Freedom of Information, which unhappily seems to have been doomed to obscurity. In its early days the Human Rights Commission was much concerned with this subject and appointed a Sub-Commission on Freedom of Information. In addition a special conference on Freedom of Information was held in 1948 at which the first draft of the Convention was adopted. This draft was referred to the General Assembly where it became bogged down in amendments and disagreements so that a final text has still not been approved. The spur to action provided by the Sub-Commission on Freedom of Information was removed in 1951 when the Sub-Commission was abolished by the Economic and Social Council, and little real progress has been made since.

The second draft, the draft Convention on the Elimination of all Forms of Intolerance and of Discrimination Based on Religion or Belief, seems to have a better chance of adoption. This draft is the result of prolonged and detailed work on the question of religious discrimination by the Sub-Commission on the Prevention of Discrimination and the Protection of Minorities. It was submitted to the General Assembly at its 1967 session but the task of examining the text in detail – which may involve amendments of substance as well as of detail – could not be completed at that session.

In the form submitted to the General Assembly the draft defines 'religion or belief' to include theistic, non-theistic and atheistic beliefs and goes on to guarantee the right to freedom of thought, conscience, religion or belief, which is stated to include:

(a) freedom to adhere or not to adhere to any religion or belief and to change his religion or belief in accordance with the dictates of his conscience without being subjected to any ... limitations ... or to any coercion likely to impair his freedom of choice or decision in the matter;
(b) freedom to manifest his religion or belief either alone or in community with others, and in public or in private, without being subjected to any discrimination on the ground of religion or belief.

In particular, the following are guaranteed:

(a) freedom to worship, to hold assemblies related to religion or belief and to establish and maintain places of worship or assembly for these purposes;

(*b*) freedom to teach, to disseminate and to learn one's religion or belief and its sacred languages or traditions, to write, print and publish religious books and texts, and to train personnel intending to devote themselves to its practices or observances;

(*c*) freedom to practise one's religion or belief by establishing and maintaining charitable and educational institutions and by expressing in public life the implications of religion or belief;

(*d*) freedom to observe the rituals, dietary and other practices of one's religion or belief and to produce or if necessary import the objects, foods and other articles and facilities customarily used in its observances and practices;

(*e*) freedom to make pilgrimages and other journeys in connexion with one's religion or belief whether inside or outside his country;

(*f*) equal legal protection for the places of worship or assembly, the rites, ceremonies and activities, and the places of disposal of the dead associated with one's religion or belief;

(*g*) freedom to organize and maintain local, regional, national and international associations in connexion with one's religion or belief, to participate in their activities, and to communicate with one's co-religionists and believers;

(*h*) freedom from compulsion to take an oath of a religious nature.

The rights of parents to bring up their children in the religion or belief of their choice are also guaranteed, and discrimination on religious grounds in the exercise of rights and freedoms is specifically prohibited.

While the fate of this draft Convention – and in particular of the measures for its implementation that have been proposed by the Sub-Commission – is still uncertain, it is earnestly to be hoped that it will be adopted in the near future.

Declarations

In addition to its work on international conventions, the General Assembly has issued a number of Declarations on important subjects which, while they are not legally binding, have exercised appreciable influence as representing the considered views of the nations of the world. The most important is, of course, the

Universal Declaration itself. The next most influential has probably been the Declaration on the Granting of Independence to Colonial Countries and Peoples, passed in 1960, which has formed the basis for all subsequent United Nations action in the colonial field. There can be no doubt that the United Nations has played a significant part in hastening the process of decolonization and the movement towards independence and the right of self-determination for all peoples.

Another important declaration was adopted recently, by the 1967 session of the General Assembly: the Declaration on Territorial Asylum, whose object is to protect persons seeking or enjoying asylum and to ensure that they shall not be returned to the state from which they have sought refuge and in which they may face persecution.

International conventions on a particular subject may be preceded or accompanied by a Declaration on the same topic. Thus, for example, the General Assembly adopted a Declaration on the Elimination of All Forms of Racial Discrimination in 1963, two years before the Convention on the same subject. In the field of religious discrimination, on the other hand, work on the draft Convention has progressed more rapidly than work on the draft Declaration.

Special studies of specific rights

A programme of studies of specific rights or groups of rights was initiated by the Human Rights Commission in 1956. One of the purposes of such a study is to obtain detailed information on the subject before deciding on a course of action, or with a view to proceeding along lines already decided upon – such as the preparation of a convention; studies are also undertaken with a view to educating world opinion.

Such studies have been undertaken in particular by the Human Rights Commission and the Sub-Commission on the Prevention of Discrimination and Protection of Minorities, but also by other organs and specialized agencies of the United Nations. They include studies of discrimination in four fields: education, political rights, religious rights and practices and the right of everyone to leave any country, including his own, and to return to his country;

a Study of the Right of Everyone to be Free from Arbitrary Arrest, Detention and Exile; and others are in preparation.

Advisory services in the field of human rights

In 1955 the General Assembly instituted a programme of advisory services in the field of human rights and authorized the Secretary-General to make provision at the request of governments for assistance in the human rights field in three forms which are designed to give governments an opportunity to share their experiences and exchange knowledge on the promotion of human rights. They are as follows:

(A) ADVISORY SERVICES OF EXPERTS. There have in fact been few requests from governments for the assistance of experts in dealing with human rights problems. None the less, two governments asked for and received advice concerning elections, electoral laws, procedures and techniques, and experts have also assisted governments on problems relating to the status of women.

(B) HUMAN RIGHTS SEMINARS. Such seminars may be organized by the Secretary-General (which in practice means by the Human Rights Division of the U.N. Secretariat) in consultation with a government which is prepared to act as host to a seminar on a suitable subject.

Such seminars have proved to be the most successful branch of the advisory services programme. They are usually organized on a regional basis and attended by persons chosen by the member governments of the region in question. Their principal purpose is to enable responsible national officials and others to exchange views and experiences on the human rights problems which are the subject of the seminar.

Seminars have considered such subjects as the protection of human rights in criminal procedure and in the administration of criminal justice; habeas corpus and other similar remedies; judicial and other remedies against the illegal exercise or abuse of administrative authority; freedom of information; the role of the police in the protection of human rights and freedom of association.

While it is not the purpose of these seminars to seek final conclusions or to assert a majority view, they do provide a valuable opportunity for the exchange of views and the broadening of the ideas that may be put into practice at the national level. The success of the programme is evidenced by the fact that since they were inaugurated some thirty seminars have been held.

(C) FELLOWSHIPS AND SCHOLARSHIPS. Since 1956 the General Assembly has made available funds for the awarding of a number of fellowships and scholarships in the human rights field as part of its programme of technical assistance. In the last few years the average annual figure for awards has been about forty.

Most human rights fellowships are granted for advanced study tours and special training. The General Assembly has directed that in the choosing of recipients regard should be paid to the 'greater needs of the under-developed areas'. Most of the fellows have been government officials of a certain standing, in the age range of twenty-five to forty-five. Among those awarded fellowships have been public prosecutors, judges, senior police officials, instructors at police academies, officials responsible for drafting legislation, officials of national development boards, of ministries of justice, labour and social affairs, and of women's bureaux, members of legislatures, officials of national non-governmental organizations, members of the bar and university teachers.

Periodic reports on human rights

In 1956 the Economic and Social Council, acting on a recommendation of the Human Rights Commission, instituted a system of periodic reports on human rights under which governments are requested to transmit to the United Nations reports describing developments and progress achieved in the human rights field. Under the system as it operates at present, these reports are submitted in a continuing three-year cycle: in the first year on civil and political rights; in the second year on economic, social and cultural rights; and in the third year on freedom of information. These reports are forwarded to the Commission on Human Rights, the Commission on the Status of Women and the Sub-Commission on the Prevention of Discrimination and the Protection of Minorities. The Human Rights Commission each year establishes a special *ad hoc* committee to study and evaluate the reports.[5]

The weakness of this system is that the reports are prepared by governments who are naturally concerned to present themselves in the best possible light. If they fail to report at all, no effective action can be taken against them. Further, there is no procedure for taking action on the basis of the reports. Some counter-balance to the information supplied by governments is provided by the fact that non-governmental organizations (like Amnesty) in consultative status with the Economic and Social Council are invited to submit comments and observations of an objective character on the situation in the field of human rights to assist the Human Rights Commission in its consideration of the governmental periodic reports. To the extent that non-governmental organizations make use of this power there is thus some information from an outside source with which the governmental reports may be compared.

Recent developments

As has already been made clear, except under the new implementation provisions contained in the Protocol to the International Covenant on Civil and Political Rights and under similar provisions in the Convention on Racial Discrimination, there is no power in the United Nations to deal with complaints, by individuals or groups, of alleged violations of human rights. None the less, large numbers of complaints (called 'communications' in U.N. terminology) are received and they are dealt with according to a procedure laid down by the Economic and Social Council in 1959. Two lists are made; the first, known as the 'non-confidential list', indicates the substance of those communications which deal with the principles involved in the promotion of universal respect for and observance of human rights; the second, confidential, list contains the substance of complaints relating to violations of human rights. These lists are furnished to the members of the Human Rights Commission; the latter list is distributed at a special meeting held in private for the

5. Reports have been considered on three occasions. Forty-one were available in 1959, sixty-one in 1961–2 and forty-eight in 1964.

purpose. If a communication refers specifically to a particular country a copy of it is communicated to the government of that country (though the identity of authors of 'Confidential' Communications is not disclosed) and any reply of that government is presented to the Commission. The members of the Commission may, on request, consult the originals of communications in the non-confidential but not in the confidential list. Under this procedure there is nothing the Commission can do about these communications other than to take note of them and there has been increasing dissatisfaction with the existing situation.

However, there have been a number of recent developments which seem to indicate that the Human Rights Commission may now be prepared to investigate violations of human rights, at least where they constitute a persistent pattern or system of conduct. These developments stem from a resolution of the Economic and Social Council of 1966 requesting the Human Rights Commission to consider as a matter of importance and urgency the question of violations of human rights and fundamental freedoms including policies of racial discrimination and apartheid in all countries, with particular reference to colonial and dependent countries.

At its session in 1967, for the first time in its history, the Commission set up a fact-finding body in the form of a Working Group of Experts, to:

(a) investigate the charges of torture and ill-treatment of prisoners, detainees or persons in police custody in South Africa;
(b) receive communications and hear witnesses and use such modalities of procedure as it may deem appropriate;
(c) recommend action to be taken in concrete cases;
(d) report to the Commission on Human Rights at the earliest possible time.

The Working Group held a number of meetings in Africa and Europe as well as at United Nations headquarters and heard twenty-five witnesses. It produced a detailed and documented report which was submitted to the 1968 session of the Human Rights Commission.

In addition to its fresh instructions to the Commission, the Economic and Social Council in 1967 asked the Sub-Commission on the Prevention of Discrimination and the Protection of Minorities to examine information relevant to gross violations of human rights and fundamental freedoms as exemplified by the policy of apartheid as practised in the Republic of South Africa and the Territory of South West Africa, and to racial discrimination as practised notably in Southern Rhodesia, and for this purpose authorized the Sub-Commission to examine the lists of communications relating to human rights referred to above.

At its 1967 session the Sub-Commission, in addition to noting the flagrant violations of human rights that are taking place in the territories referred to by ECOSOC and in the Portuguese overseas territories, drew the attention of the Human Rights Commission to

Some particularly glaring examples of situations which reveal consistent patterns of violations of human rights and regarding which the Sub-Commission has expressed its unanimous views in the course of its discussions:

(a) the situation in Greece, resulting from the arbitrary arrest, detention and ill-treatment of political prisoners, and the denials of human rights involved, for example, in censorship and prohibition on the rights of assembly and free speech, since the *coup d'état* of 21 April 1967; and

(b) the situation in Haiti, resulting from the arbitrary arrest and detention of political prisoners.

The Sub-Commission recommended that a Working Group of Experts, similar to that established to investigate prison conditions in South Africa, should be set up to examine these situations.

At its 1968 session, however, the Human Rights Commission, while keeping in being the Working Group of Experts already established and extending its mandate to include prison conditions in South West Africa, Southern Rhodesia and the Portuguese colonies, decided to take no further action on other violations of human rights. None the less, the initiative taken has set a precedent that is capable of expansion in the future if the will is there.

Limitations on effective U.N. action

In considering the limited achievements of the United Nations in the field of human rights it is important to bear in mind that in the last resort the United Nations consists, in effect, of the governments of the member states, and that it cannot give itself powers which those governments are not prepared to grant or undertake activities to which those governments do not consent. Any reproaches and criticisms should rather be directed at governments than at the United Nations itself.

It is understandable – though regrettable – that governments are reluctant to allow outside supervision and control (or interference as they would call it) of activities which may violate the rights and freedoms of their citizens. Yet if human rights are to be effectively protected it is essential that in the last resort the individual whose rights have been violated by his government should be able to appeal to an independent outside body.

The first steps have been taken towards the establishment of such a body with the International Covenant on Civil and Political Rights which provides for a Human Rights Committee in the form already described, and with the International Convention on Racial Discrimination, which provides for a Committee on Racial Discrimination, with powers similar to those of the Human Rights Committee but limited to complaints of racial discrimination.

The weaknesses of this system of implementation machinery consisting of special committees for each convention – and a similar committee is proposed for the Draft Convention on Religious Intolerance – are several. In the first place, it is piecemeal and disjointed; secondly, it is political rather than judicial; thirdly it can only come into operation on the complaint of an individual if the government against which he wishes to make a complaint has recognized the right of individual complaint; and finally, the committee which investigates the complaint can make no binding or enforceable decision – it cannot even publish its findings or views, let alone ensure that they are implemented.

What is needed is an international court of human rights established according to judicial norms and following a judicial procedure, with jurisdiction to pronounce on violations of human rights, to which any individual who alleges that a right guaranteed him under any binding international instrument has been violated can bring his complaint.

A further weakness of the present system of providing international protection of human rights by means of conventions is that a convention is not, once adopted, automatically binding upon the states which voted for it. It only binds those states which have ratified it. Ratification is a formal procedure which may be carried out either by the government or the parliament of a state, depending on that state's internal laws. Thus the International Covenants on Human Rights are not yet in force, for to enter into force – i.e. even to bind those states which have ratified it – a convention must have been ratified by a minimum number of states, as specified in the Convention itself. Thus the International Covenants on Human Rights require a minimum of thirty-five ratifications before entering into force at all.

Implementation machinery for the protection of human rights generally at the United Nations level is thus still a thing of the future, and is likely to remain so as long as governments are not prepared to make the concessions necessary to make it a reality.

Proposal for a U.N. High Commissioner for Human Rights

There is at present before the United Nations a proposal for the establishment of a United Nations High Commissioner for Human Rights, with a status somewhat analogous to the High Commissioner for Refugees. This proposal, if adopted, will provide the United Nations with a modest but useful instrument for extending its work in the human rights field.

The High Commissioner is not intended to form part of the machinery for the implementation of existing or future international instruments relating to human rights, and his powers and functions will not be such as to clash with any existing or future machinery for their implementation, but will be complementary to such machinery. He will in particular have power to advise and to comment on human rights questions.

The High Commissioner's power to give advice and assistance to United Nations organs which request it will be of considerable value to bodies such as the Commission on Human Rights, which is limited in the activities it can undertake by its structure and the occasional nature of its meetings. Further, the High Commissioner, being independent of government influence, would be in a position to act completely impartially in any assistance he might give to United Nations organs.

The High Commissioner, through his annual report to the General Assembly, could play an important part in encouraging and securing the ratification of international conventions relating to human rights and in drawing attention to fields in which action is needed.

At the same time the High Commissioner's proposed powers are so defined and limited that his office will in no way encroach upon national sovereignty. He would not be able to intervene in the internal affairs of any state, nor undertake an investigation against the will of the state concerned, but only to act in relation to the internal affairs of a state if he were requested to render assistance by the government of that state. These limitations make the proposal more acceptable to states than a proposal for a High Commissioner with greater powers would be, and it must be hoped that it will be adopted, for the High Commissioner would make a useful contribution to the protection of human rights.

2. THE COUNCIL OF EUROPE

The Council of Europe is a regional organization with a present membership of eighteen states (Austria, Belgium, Cyprus, Denmark, France, Federal Republic of Germany, Greece, Iceland, Ireland, Italy, Luxembourg, Malta, Netherlands, Norway, Sweden, Switzerland, Turkey and the United Kingdom). It has two organs: an inter-governmental body, the Committee of Ministers, consisting of the Ministers of Foreign Affairs of the member states – which is the only body with decision-making powers – and a parliamentary body, the Consultative Assembly, which consists of 147 members representing the parliaments of the member states, and which has a purely deliberative function.

One of the aims of the Council of Europe – which was set up to achieve greater unity between its members – is cooperation in 'the maintenance and further realization of human rights and fundamental freedoms'. Article 3 of the Statute provides that every member of the Council of Europe must accept the principles of the rule of law and the enjoyment by all persons within its jurisdiction of human rights and fundamental freedoms. The maintenance of human rights and fundamental freedoms is thus not only one of the objectives of the organization, it is actually a condition of membership. This is one of the main reasons why Spain and Portugal have not been admitted to membership, and why the military take-over in Greece has been followed by proposals for the expulsion of Greece.

The Council of Europe is the only body that has thus far taken effective action to set up an international body of judicial character to investigate allegations of violations of human rights. This has been done by means of the *European Convention for the Protection of Human Rights and Fundamental Freedoms,* which was adopted in November 1950 and entered into force on 3 September 1953 when it had been ratified by ten states; it has now been ratified by sixteen of the eighteen member states (all except France and Switzerland).

The European Convention takes as its point of departure the Universal Declaration of Human Rights and states in the preamble that the contracting parties are resolved 'to take the first steps for the collective enforcement of certain of the rights stated in the Universal Declaration'. Among the rights thus protected by the European Convention are freedom of conscience and religion, and freedom of opinion and expression. Before going into the precise form in which these rights are protected, it is important to outline the procedure by which that protection is made effective.

For this purpose the Convention establishes two organs, the European Commission of Human Rights and the European Court of Human Rights, which are responsible for ensuring 'the observance of the engagements undertaken by the High Contracting Parties'.

THE EUROPEAN COMMISSION OF HUMAN RIGHTS

came into being on 3 September 1953 when the convention came into force. It consists of a number of members equal to the number of the states who have ratified the Convention, elected by the Committee of Ministers from a list of names drawn up by the Bureau of the Consultative Assembly from names proposed by each group of parliamentary representatives in the Assembly, who are themselves elected by each of the parliaments of the member states from among their members. They are thus not government nominees; while they are formally *appointed* by the governmental organ of the Council of Europe, they are *proposed* for appointment by the parliamentary organ; and their independence of their government is thus assured.

The Commission has power to investigate alleged violations by a contracting state of any of the rights protected by the Convention. Petitions alleging such a violation may be made by an individual, non-governmental organization or group of individuals if the state against which the complaint is made has made a declaration recognizing the Commission's competence to receive individual petitions. Eleven of the sixteen contracting states have recognized this right of individual petition (Austria, Belgium, Denmark, Federal Republic of Germany, Iceland, Ireland, Luxembourg, Netherlands, Norway, Sweden and the United Kingdom). This right is undoubtedly the key element in the structure set up by the European Convention. Its importance is evidenced by the fact that over 3,000 individual applications have been received so far as opposed to four applications by states – *Austria v. Italy* alleging violations in the South Tyrol in respect of the German-speaking population there; *Greece v. United Kingdom* alleging violations in Cyprus before independence (two cases); and the present application of *Denmark, Netherlands, Norway and Sweden v. Greece* alleging wholesale violations of the Convention by the military régime. Individual applications have related to a wide range of matters including the length of pre-trial detention, the right to a fair trial, alleged 'inhuman treatment' and the rights of minorities, as well as freedom of conscience and religion and freedom of opinion and expression.

The procedure of the Commission – while it does not lead to a judicial decision – is essentially judicial in character in the sense that all the judicial guarantees are respected: the right to be legally represented, the right of reply, and, if appropriate, an oral hearing and the taking of the testimony of witnesses in the presence of both sides. The purpose of the procedure before the Commission is in the first instance to examine the receivability of the complaint (i.e. to see whether it falls within the provisions of the Convention) and then, if it is found to be receivable, to establish the facts and to attempt by conciliation to achieve a friendly settlement of the case.

If the Commission is unable to effect a settlement it draws up a report in which it sets out the facts and gives its opinion as to whether those facts disclose a breach of the Convention. This report is transmitted to the parties to the case and to the Committee of Ministers. While the opinion of the Commission is not binding on the state concerned, it is of considerable influence and may well induce the state to take appropriate action to rectify the situation. If it does not do so, there are two possibilities: the case may be referred to the European Court of Human Rights for a judicial decision;[1] if this is not done, it is for the Committee of Ministers to take a final decision on the case.

THE EUROPEAN COURT OF HUMAN RIGHTS

was constituted on 20 April 1958 and met to consider its first case in October 1960. It consists of a number of judges equal to that of the members of the Council of Europe, i.e. at present eighteen. They are elected by the Consultative Assembly from a list of candidates submitted by the member states.

The Court is not automatically competent to hear a case. While a state may agree that any particular dispute be referred to the Court, for a case to be referred without the consent of the state concerned that state must have made a declaration accepting the automatic jurisdiction of the Court. Eleven States have done so – the same as have recognized the right of individual petition to the

1. Provided the state complained against has accepted the Court's jurisdiction – see below.

Commission. The four cases decided by the Court have related to the legality of detention without trial under emergency regulations (in Ireland), the length of pre-trial detention (in Austria and Germany) and the rights of members of a minority group to have their children educated in their mother-tongue (Belgium).

In no cases may individuals refer a case to the Court. The power to do so is reserved to the Commission itself and to the contracting states.

The procedure before the Court is, of course, of a judicial nature. The starting point is formed by the Commission's report on the case, and the proceedings are normally divided into two parts: a written stage and a subsequent oral hearing. An individual applicant who has brought a case before the Commission cannot be directly represented before the Court if his case is subsequently referred to it; his interests and his point of view are represented by the Commission – which may place his observations before the Court – and he may be heard as a witness; but he is not a party to the proceedings.

In its judgment the Court gives a decision as to whether or not there has been a violation of the Convention and gives its reasons. It may also, where appropriate, 'afford just satisfaction to the injured party'. Its judgment is final and binding on the parties to the case, which must give effect to it. Its execution is supervised by the Committee of Ministers, which would be responsible for deciding on appropriate action against a recalcitrant state which refused or failed to implement a judgment of the Court.

THE COMMITTEE OF MINISTERS

may also be called upon to take enforcement action (though it has not yet had to do so) if a case investigated by the Commission is not referred to the Court. In such cases it takes it decisions by a two-thirds majority (as opposed to the need for unanimity on other important decisions). If the Committee of Ministers decides in a particular case that there has been a violation of the Convention, it prescribes a period during which the state concerned must take remedial measures. If no such measures are taken, the Committee must then decide 'what effect shall be given to its original decision'. No indication is given in the Convention of the nature of the steps that could be taken by the Committee, other than the publication of the Commission's report. In practice, however, the states parties to the Convention have undertaken by the Convention itself to conform to a decision of the Committee of Ministers and may be expected to do so. The ultimate sanction available to the Committee of Ministers would seem to be expulsion from the Council of Europe.

FREEDOM OF CONSCIENCE AND RELIGION UNDER THE CONVENTION

By Article 9 of the European Convention:

(1) Everyone has the right to freedom of thought, conscience and religion; this right includes freedom to change his religion or belief and freedom either alone or in community with others and in public or private, to manifest his religion or belief, in worship, teaching, practice and observance.

(2) Freedom to manifest one's religion or beliefs shall be subject only to such limitations as are prescribed by law and are necessary in a democratic society in the interests of public safety, for the protection of public order, health or morals, or for the protection of the rights and freedoms of others.

The effects of Article 9 on the law of the states parties to the Convention can be illustrated by two instances. In Norway Article 2 of the Constitution, which dated from 1814, banned the Jesuits within the country. Under the influence of the provisions of the Convention, Norway amended the Constitution so as to withdraw the ban and thus comply fully with the provisions of Article 9. In Belgium, Article 9 was directly applied in the case of Cymerman, a practising Jew who was unemployed. The regulations required him to report at the Employment Office for six consecutive days before he could draw unemployment benefit. He failed to report on the Saturday and when he was refused payment as a result he appealed on the ground that Article 9 of the Convention guaranteed him the right to practise his religion, which forbade him to undertake any secular activities on a Saturday. This argument was accepted and his claim to unemployment benefit was allowed on appeal.

So far as applications to the European Commission on Human Rights under Article 9 are concerned, the only important issue that has been raised has been the question of conscientious objection to military service and whether compulsory military service or alternative service violates the right to freedom of conscience. The only case decided so far has been *Grandrath v. Federal Republic of Germany* in which a Jehovah's Witness, who had been accepted as a conscientious objector, was sentenced to six months' imprisonment for refusing to perform alternative service. Both the Commission and the Committee of Ministers took the view that there had not been a violation of the Convention in this particular case.

The question of conscientious objection has also been taken up at other levels of the Council of Europe and is at present under active consideration. It was on the initiative of a non-governmental organization that this question was first raised, when Amnesty International, which has consultative status with the Council of Europe, proposed in September 1965 that the subject of the right of conscientious objection be placed on the agenda of the Consultative Assembly. The Bureau of the Assembly referred the matter to the Legal Committee of the Consultative Assembly with a view to examining the possibility of securing the adoption of a recommendation or resolution on the subject.

After the question had been discussed and examined at length by the Legal Committee, it was debated in the Consultative Assembly in January 1967 and a resolution was adopted by the Assembly on the 26 January of that year in which the following basic principles were affirmed:

Persons liable to conscription for military service who, for reasons of conscience or profound conviction arising from religious, ethical, moral, humanitarian, philosophical or similar motives, refuse to perform armed service shall enjoy a personal right to be released from the obligation to perform such service.

This right shall be regarded as deriving logically from the fundamental rights of the individual in democratic Rule of Law states which are guaranteed in Article 9 of the European Convention on Human Rights.

The resolution went on to lay down principles applicable to the procedure for granting the right of conscientious objection and for alternative service.

On the basis of this resolution the Consultative Assembly instructed its Legal Committee to report regularly to it on measures taken in pursuance of its terms and recommended the Committee of Ministers (*a*) to instruct the Committee of Experts on Human Rights (a body set up within the framework of the Council of Europe to study and advise on human rights questions) to formulate proposals to give effect to the principles laid down in the resolution by means of a convention or a recommendation to governments so that the right of conscientious objection may be firmly implanted in all member states of the Council of Europe; and (*b*) to invite member states to bring their national legislation as closely as possible into line with the principles adopted by the Consultative Assembly.

This latest initiative has not yet resulted in concrete proposals, but the matter is under active consideration and it is to be hoped that it will result in the adoption of a measure formally protecting the right of conscientious objection.

FREEDOM OF OPINION AND EXPRESSION UNDER THE CONVENTION

Article 10 of the European Convention reads as follows:

(1) Everyone has the right to freedom of expression. This right shall include freedom to hold opinions and to receive and impart information and ideas without interference by public authority and regardless of frontiers. This Article shall not prevent States from requiring the licensing of broadcasting, television or cinema enterprises.

(2) The exercise of these freedoms, since it carries with it duties and responsibilities, may be subject to such formalities, conditions, restrictions or penalties as are prescribed by law and are necessary in a democratic society, in the interests of national security, territorial integrity or public safety, for the prevention of disorder or crime, for the protection of health or morals, for the protection of the reputation or rights of others, for preventing the disclosing of information received in confidence, or for maintaining the authority and impartiality of the judiciary.

Among applications made under Article 10 of the Convention it is proposed to describe only one, which was one of the few cases to be referred to the Court. The case of *de Becker v. Belgium* was an individual application brought by a Belgian journalist who on conviction after the war of the offence of collaborating with the enemy was made subject to an order prohibiting him from writing or publishing. He complained to the European Commission that this prohibition interfered with the freedom of expression guaranteed him under the European Convention. The Commission upheld this view and expressed the opinion that the provisions of the Belgian criminal law under which the prohibition had been imposed were not fully justifiable under the Convention

in so far as the deprivation of freedom of expression in regard to non-political matters, which they contain, is imposed inflexibly for life without any provision for its relaxation when, with the passage of time, public morale and public order have been re-established and the continued imposition of that particular incapacity has ceased to be a measure 'necessary in a democratic society' within the meaning of Article 10 (2) of the Convention.

The case was then referred to the Court, but before any formal decision was reached the Belgian legislature amended the relevant legislation in a manner satisfactory both to de Becker and to the European Commission, and the case was withdrawn at that stage on the basis that the provisions of the European Convention were no longer violated.

The importance of the role of the Commission – an independent, international body – in interpreting the provisions of the Convention, and in particular those which allow restrictions on rights in certain defined circumstances, is vividly illustrated in this case. The dangers of abuse involved in allowing governments to impose restrictions on the exercise of fundamental rights are much reduced when it is not the government which decides whether the circumstances justifying a restriction are present, but an independent and judicial body.

THE INTER-AMERICAN COMMISSION ON HUMAN RIGHTS

Cooperation between the states of America in the human rights field began as early as 1945 when the Conference of American States held in Mexico asked the Inter-American Juridical Committee to prepare an American Declaration of the Rights and Duties of Man. In 1948 the ninth Conference of American States, held in Bogota, created the Organization of American States, and the same conference adopted the American Declaration of the Rights and Duties of Man according to which 'the international protection of the rights of man should be the principal guide of an evolving American Law'.

While proposals for an Inter-American Convention on Human Rights are still at the draft stage, an Inter-American Commission on Human Rights was established by the Ministers of Foreign Affairs of the O.A.S. in 1959. It is composed of seven members elected in their personal capacity by the O.A.S. Council from a list of candidates proposed by the member states.

Article 1 of the statute of the Commission states that its function is 'to promote respect for human rights'. Its powers are defined in more detail in Article 9 as follows:

(a) To develop an awareness of human rights among the peoples of America;

(b) To make recommendations to the governments of the member states in general, if it considers such action advisable, for the adoption of progressive measures in favor of human rights within the framework of their domestic legislation and, in accordance with their constitutional precepts, appropriate measures to further the faithful observance of those rights;

(c) To prepare such studies or reports as it considers advisable in the performance of its duties;

(d) To urge the governments of the member states to supply it with information on the measures adopted by them in matters of human rights.

Under these powers the Commission has undertaken two important forms of activity: the preparation of studies and the conduct of inquiries.

Among the studies carried out has been one leading to the preparation by the Commission of a draft Convention on Freedom of Expression, Information and Research, which is now being examined by the member states of the O.A.S.

The Commission has considered itself empowered by its Statute to conduct inquiries into alleged violations of human rights in the American states, although it recognizes that it has no power to take decisions. In doing so, it takes as its point of departure the American Declaration of the Rights and Duties of Man, on the provisions of which its activities are based.

The Commission has laid down a regular procedure for examining petitions that it receives alleging violations of human rights. A preliminary examination is carried out in order to decide whether the petition is admissible. If it is, it is communicated to the state concerned which is invited to put its case, which in turn is communicated to the petitioner. The petitioner may ask to be heard in person by the Commission.

Until recently the Commission could carry its investigation into individual complaints no further; it did, however, evolve a procedure for dealing with complaints which appear to indicate a systematic course of conduct. If the Commission receives a large number of petitions against a particular country which appear to be of substance, and as to which no satisfactory reply is made, it may decide to conduct an inquiry. As a first step the secretariat prepares a study of the human rights situation in that country, and the Commission itself then seeks the permission of the country concerned to establish the facts by an on-the-spot inquiry. A number of such inquiries have been held, for example in the Dominican Republic after the fall of Trujillo and at the time of the United States' landing of paratroopers, and in Ecuador at the recent elections; in other cases (for example Cuba and Haiti) permission has been refused by the government concerned. In the course of inquiry the Commission requests information from the government and hears the evidence of anyone who wishes to appear before it. It then draws up a report on the human rights situation in the country in question. If appropriate, it may make recommendations of a general character to the government of that country. These reports and recommendations may be published if the Commission so decides, and for this reason their influence can be considerable.

In addition the Commission may now make recommendations to governments on individual petitions in certain cases. This extended power of the Commission was decided upon at the second Extraordinary Inter-American Conference held in Rio de Janeiro in 1965, and was incorporated into its statute in 1966. This new procedure relates only to petitions alleging infringements of one of the following rights: right to life, freedom and security, equality before the law, freedom of religion, research, opinion, expression, information, right to a fair trial, freedom from arbitrary arrest and the right to legal safeguards. In respect of such petitions the Commission must first satisfy itself that all available domestic remedies have been exhausted. It then examines the complaint and invites the government concerned to provide all relevant information. If it finds the complaint justified the Commission may make appropriate recommendations to the government concerned, 'with a view to the more effective protection of human rights'.

If a government does not comply with the recommendations of the Commission, two possible sanctions are provided for. In the first place, the Commission may comment upon the matter in its annual report to the Inter-American Conference or the Consultative Meeting of Foreign Ministers. If these bodies do not make any comments upon the recommendations of the Commission it may then publish its report.

It is to be expected that this important step forward, which was brought into operation in May 1967, will considerably increase the role that the Inter-American Commission is already playing in the protection of human rights in the Americas. This role is illustrated by the fact that by the end of 1967 it had examined about 4,000 petitions and that in the first year of operation of the new procedure it was applied in forty-four cases. The Commission has conducted inquiries into eight countries and drawn attention to developments in others. It has published many comprehensive reports and the value of its contribution is unquestionable.

CONCLUSION

Perhaps the most striking thing to emerge from this study of international action for the protection of human rights is that positive achievements are much easier at the regional level than at the universal level. This is perhaps not surprising since any form of international action depends upon agreement being reached between governments, and such agreement is clearly easier among states of a particular region which usually have a great deal in common, both in the nature of the problems they face and in their attitude to the solution of those problems.

Progress at the United Nations level has been slow because general agreement among the nations of the world is almost impossible of achievement; and also because governments are extremely reluctant to agree to anything that would involve a limitation on their freedom to act as they wish without control or restraint.

None the less there has been some progress and some abandonment of the concept of absolute national sovereignty in favour of the right of the individual to complain to an international body if his fundamental rights are violated by his government. It is essential that this progress should be maintained. What is needed is, in the first instance, a series of regional organizations such as those already existing in western Europe and America – Human Rights Commissions for Asia, Africa, eastern Europe, the Middle East – and at the universal level a World Commission of Human Rights and a World Court of Human Rights to which any individual unable to obtain redress at the national or regional levels could bring his complaint. Such a structure will take time and patience to achieve, but it must be the ultimate aim of all those concerned with the protection of human rights.

Universal Declaration
of Human Rights

On 10 December 1948 the General Assembly of the United Nations adopted and proclaimed the Universal Declaration of Human Rights, the full text of which appears in the following pages. Following this historic act the Assembly called upon all Member countries to publicize the text of the Declaration and 'to cause it to be disseminated, displayed, read and expounded principally in schools and other educational institutions, without distinction based on the political status of countries or territories.'

Final Authorized Text

UNITED NATIONS

OFFICE OF PUBLIC INFORMATION

PREAMBLE

Whereas recognition of the inherent dignity and of the equal and inalienable rights of all members of the human family is the foundation of freedom, justice and peace in the world,

Whereas disregard and contempt for human rights have resulted in barbarous acts which have outraged the conscience of mankind, and the advent of a world in which human beings shall enjoy freedom of speech and belief and freedom from fear and want has been proclaimed as the highest aspiration of the common people,

Whereas it is essential, if man is not to be compelled to have recourse, as a last resort, to rebellion against tyranny and oppression, that human rights should be protected by the rule of law,

Whereas it is essential to promote the development of friendly relations between nations,

Whereas the peoples of the United Nations have in the Charter reaffirmed their faith in fundamental human rights, in the dignity and worth of the human person and in the equal rights of men and women and have determined to promote social progress and better standards of life in larger freedom,

Whereas Member States have pledged themselves to achieve, in cooperation with the United Nations, the promotion of universal respect for and observance of human rights and fundamental freedoms,

Whereas a common understanding of these rights and freedoms is of the greatest importance for the full realization of this pledge.

Now, therefore, the General Assembly proclaims this Universal Declaration of Human Rights as a common standard of achievement for all peoples and all nations, to the end that every individual and every organ of society, keeping this Declaration constantly in mind, shall strive by teaching and education to promote respect for these rights and freedoms and by progressive measures, national and international, to secure their universal and effective recognition and observance, both among the peoples of Member States themselves and among the peoples of territories under their jurisdiction.

Article 1. All human beings are born free and equal in dignity and rights. They are endowed with reason and conscience and should act towards one another in a spirit of brotherhood.

Article 2. Everyone is entitled to all the rights and freedoms set forth in this Declaration, without distinction of any kind, such as race, colour, sex, language, religion, political or other opinion, national or social origin, property, birth or other status.

Furthermore, no distinction shall be made on the basis of the political, jurisdictional or international status of the country or territory to which a person belongs, whether it be independent, trust, non-self-governing or under any other limitation of sovereignty.

Article 3. Everyone has the right to life, liberty and security of person.

Article 4. No one shall be held in slavery or servitude; slavery and the slave trade shall be prohibited in all their forms.

Article 5. No one shall be subjected to torture or to cruel, inhuman or degrading treatment or punishment.

Article 6. Everyone has the right to recognition everywhere as a person before the law.

Article 7. All are equal before the law and are entitled without any discrimination to equal protection of the law. All are entitled to equal protection against any discrimination in violation of this Declaration and against any incitement to such discrimination.

Article 8. Everyone has the right to an effective remedy by the competent national tribunals for acts violating the fundamental rights granted him by the constitution or by law.

Article 9. No one shall be subjected to arbitrary arrest, detention or exile.

Article 10. Everyone is entitled in full equality to a fair and public hearing by an independent and impartial tribunal, in the determination of his rights and obligations and of any criminal charge against him.

Article 11. (1) Everyone charged with a penal offence has the right to be presumed innocent until proved guilty according to law in a public trial at which he has had all the guarantees necessary for his defence.

(2) No one shall be held guilty of any penal offence on account of any act or omission which did not constitute a penal offence, under national or international law, at the time when it was committed. Nor shall a heavier penalty be imposed than the one that was applicable at the time the penal offence was committed.

Article 12. No one shall be subjected to arbitrary interference with his privacy, family, home or correspondence, nor to attacks upon his honour and reputation. Everyone has the right to the protection of the law against such interference or attacks.

Article 13. (1) Everyone has the right to freedom of movement and residence within the borders of each state.

(2) Everyone has the right to leave any country, including his own, and to return to his country.

Article 14. (1) Everyone has the right to seek and to enjoy in other countries asylum from persecution.

(2) This right may not be invoked in the case of prosecutions genuinely arising from non-political crimes or from acts contrary to the purposes and principles of the United Nations.

Article 15. (1) Everyone has the right to a nationality.

(2) No one shall be arbitrarily deprived of his nationality nor denied the right to change his nationality.

Article 16. (1) Men and women of full age, without any limitation due to race, nationality or religion, have the right to marry and to found a family. They are entitled to equal rights as to marriage, during marriage and at its dissolution.

(2) Marriage shall be entered into only with the free and full consent of the intending spouses.

(3) The family is the natural and fundamental group unit of society and is entitled to protection by society and the State.

Article 17. (1) Everyone has the right to own property alone as well as in association with others.

(2) No one shall be arbitrarily deprived of his property.

Article 18. Everyone has the right to freedom of thought, conscience and religion; this right includes freedom to change his religion or belief, and freedom, either alone or in community with others and in public or private, to manifest his religion or belief in teaching, practice, worship and observance.

Article 19. Everyone has the right to freedom of opinion and expression; this right includes freedom to hold opinions without interference and to seek, receive and impart information and ideas through any media and regardless of frontiers.

Article 20. (1) Everyone has the right to freedom of peaceful assembly and association.

(2) No one may be compelled to belong to an association.

Article 21. (1) Everyone has the right to take part in the government of his country, directly or through freely chosen representatives.

(2) Everyone has the right of equal access to public service in his country.

(3) The will of the people shall be the basis of the authority of government; this will shall be expressed in periodic and genuine elections which shall be by universal and equal suffrage and shall be held by secret vote or by equivalent free voting procedures.

Article 22. Everyone, as a member of society, has the right to social security and is entitled to realization, through national effort and international cooperation and in accordance with the organization and resources of each State, of the economic, social and cultural rights indispensable for his dignity and the free development of his personality.

Article 23. (1) Everyone has the right to work, to free choice of employment, to just and favourable conditions of work and to protection against unemployment.

(2) Everyone, without any discrimination, has the right to equal pay for equal work.

(3) Everyone who works has the right to just and favourable remuneration ensuring for himself and his family an existence

worthy of human dignity, and supplemented, if necessary, by other means of social protection.

(4) Everyone has the right to form and to join trade unions for the protection of his interests.

Article 24. Everyone has the right to rest and leisure, including reasonable limitation of working hours and periodic holidays with pay.

Article 25. (1) Everyone has the right to a standard of living adequate for the health and well-being of himself and of his family, including food, clothing, housing and medical care and necessary social services, and the right to security in the event of unemployment, sickness, disability, widowhood, old age or other lack of livelihood in circumstances beyond his control.

(2) Motherhood and childhood are entitled to special care and assistance. All children, whether born in or out of wedlock, shall enjoy the same social protection.

Article 26. (1) Everyone has the right to education. Education shall be free, at least in the elementary and fundamental stages. Elementary education shall be compulsory. Technical and professional education shall be made generally available and higher education shall be equally accessible to all on the basis of merit.

(2) Education shall be directed to the full development of the human personality and to the strengthening of respect for human rights and fundamental freedoms. It shall promote understanding, tolerance and friendship among all nations, racial or religious groups, and shall further the activities of the United Nations for the maintenance of peace.

(3) Parents have a prior right to choose the kind of education that shall be given to their children.

Article 27. (1) Everyone has the right freely to participate in the cultural life of the community, to enjoy the arts and to share in scientific advancement and its benefits.

(2) Everyone has the right to the protection of the moral and material interests resulting from any scientific, literary or artistic production of which he is the author.

Article 28. Everyone is entitled to a social and international order in which the rights and freedoms set forth in this Declaration can be fully realized.

Article 29. (1) Everyone has duties to the community in which alone the free and full development of his personality is possible.

(2) In the exercise of his rights and freedoms, everyone shall be subject only to such limitations as are determined by law solely for the purpose of securing due recognition and respect for the rights and freedoms of others and of meeting the just requirements of morality, public order and the general welfare in a democratic society.

(3) These rights and freedoms may in no case be exercised contrary to the purposes and principles of the United Nations.

Article 30. Nothing in this Declaration may be interpreted as implying for any State, group or person any right to engage in any activity or to perform any act aimed at the destruction of any of the rights and freedoms set forth herein.

Notes on Contributors

MALCOLM CALDWELL, the author of two books on South East Asia, teaches the economic history of that region at the School of Oriental and African Studies, University of London. He is also Chairman of C.N.D. Born in Scotland in 1931 and educated at the universities of Edinburgh and Nottingham, he is now married and has four children.

G. NAUDÉ is a South African writer now living abroad. She has never been prominent politically, but has a strong and long-standing interest in South African law and has been able to maintain contact with many people who are banned and to gain an understanding of how the South African legislation has dealt with them.

PETER REDDAWAY is a Lecturer in Government at the London School of Economics. He gained his M.A. degree from Cambridge University, then studied as a graduate at Harvard, Moscow and the L.S.E. He has edited *Soviet Short Stories Volume 2* (Penguin, 1968), *Lenin: the Man, the Theorist, the Leader – a Reappraisal* (with Leonard Schapiro, 1967), and *Russia's Other Intellectuals: Socio-Political Writing in the Underground* (1969), and his book, *The Politics of Soviet Literature: an Historical Sketch*, is forthcoming.

PATRICIA MAY has been a practising barrister since 1966, working mainly on criminal cases. She joined Amnesty in 1963 and has since done voluntary work for that organization in numerous capacities. Born in 1940, she graduated in Law from King's College, London, and, after an L.C.C. administration course, joined the Central Council of Probation Committee. In 1965–6 she was organizing secretary to the International Conference on S.W. Africa. She is married and has a son.

HILARY CARTWRIGHT was called to the Bar in 1959 and practised as a barrister until 1965. She was then a legal officer with the International Commission of Jurists in Geneva until 1968. She has been actively associated with Amnesty International since its foundation.

MORE ABOUT PENGUINS

Penguinews, which appears every month, contains details of all the new books issued by Penguins as they are published. From time to time it is supplemented by *Penguins in Print* – a complete list of all our available titles. (There are well over three thousand of these.)

A specimen copy of *Penguinews* will be sent to you free on request, and you can become a subscriber for the price of the postage – 4s. for a year's issues (including the complete lists). Just write to Dept EP, Penguin Books Ltd, Harmondsworth, Middlesex, enclosing a cheque or postal order, and your name will be added to the mailing list.

Some other Penguin Specials are described overleaf.

Note: *Penguinews* and *Penguins in Print*
are not available in the U.S.A. or Canada

SOME RECENT PENGUIN SPECIALS

THE DEVOLUTION OF POWER
Local Democracy, Regionalism and Nationalism
J. P. Mackintosh

'Over the next few years his book could well be a basic text for one of
the most crucial debates in British politics' – *Observer*

ISRAEL AND THE ARABS *Maxime Robinson*

This analysis, written by a Jewish academic, is probably the most
devastating exposure ever made of the Zionist State in Palestine

STUDENT POWER: Problems, Diagnosis, Action
Alexander Cockburn and Robin Blackburn

Students have piecemeal grievances over discipline, grants, syllabuses
– but do they amount to a coherent structural critique of modern
society? And what are their alternatives, their plans, and their strategy
for the future?

MATTERS OF PRINCIPLE: Labour's Last Chance

Seven distinguished academics (including Tyrrell Burgess, Peter
Calvocoressi, and John Rex) examine the recent record of the Labour
Government and call for a return to certain basic principles which
have been ditched in favour of expediency and the consensus

*AMERICA: THE MIXED CURSE *Andrew Kopkind*

Trenchant essays on modern American politics by the brilliant young
American correspondent of the *New Statesman*

*OBSOLETE COMMUNISM: The Left-Wing Alternative
Gabriel and Daniel Cohn-Bendit

The polemical treatise of Danny le Rouge, the man who emerged to
lead the student revolutionaries in the dramatic 'French Revolution
1968'

*NOT FOR SALE IN THE U.S.A.